The story of

COMPTON BISHOP

and

CROSS

by

Margaret Jordan

with illustrations by
Don Osmond

First Published in 1994

Copyright © Margaret Jordan 1994

Published by R A & M Jordan, Riverton House,
Old Coach Road, Cross, Axbridge, Somerset. BS26 2EJ

Typeset and layout by Beech Nuts - DTP
Shipham, Winscombe

Printed by Bigwood and Staple, Bridgwater

ISBN 0 9523486 16 (Hardback)
ISBN 0 9523486 08 (Softback)

ACKNOWLEDGEMENTS

The author would like to thank the following:- David Bromwich, Local History Library Taunton; The staff at the County Records Office Taunton; Phillip Stoyle and staff, reference department Bridgwater Library; Warwickshire County Records Office, Warwick; Lady Elizabeth Hamilton; Frank Jarmaney; Axbridge Museum; Mary Prowse; Russ Day; The State Library of Victoria, Australia; Dr. Michael Costen; Northamptonshire County Records Office; John Bentley; Tom Mayberry; John and Jane Craig for proof reading and typing.

ACKNOWLEDGEMENTS FOR PHOTOGRAPHS

The British Museum 6; Michael Harvard 10 & 11; Glasgow Museum, The Burrell Collection 12; Michael Andrews 4, 8, 19, 27 & 35; Leicestershire Museum, Arts and Records Service 22; Christine Clark, Victoria, Australia 48 & 49; Somerset County Records Office 20, 50 & 51; Woodspring Library, Weston-super-Mare 29; Clifford Tilley 33 & 34; Axbridge Museum 32 & 36; Imperial War Museum 46; Mary Wills 39, 40 & 41; Pam Line 23, 42, 43, 44 & 45; Mrs. Slim who kindly gave several photographs of the children at Webbington House two of which are numbers 37 and 38 in this book.

I owe a special debt of thanks to the many people, too numerous to mention, who live or have lived in Compton Bishop and Cross who have generously shared their time and their memories with me.

Margaret Jordan

CONTENTS

Introduction 1

LANDSCAPE AND FEATURES 3

THE MANOR 13

THE COACH ROAD 23

COMMUNITY LIFE 37

WITHIN LIVING MEMORY 79

Appendix A; Local Surnames 89

Appendix B; Census Information 90

List of Photographs 91

Notes 93

Bibliography 94

Index 97

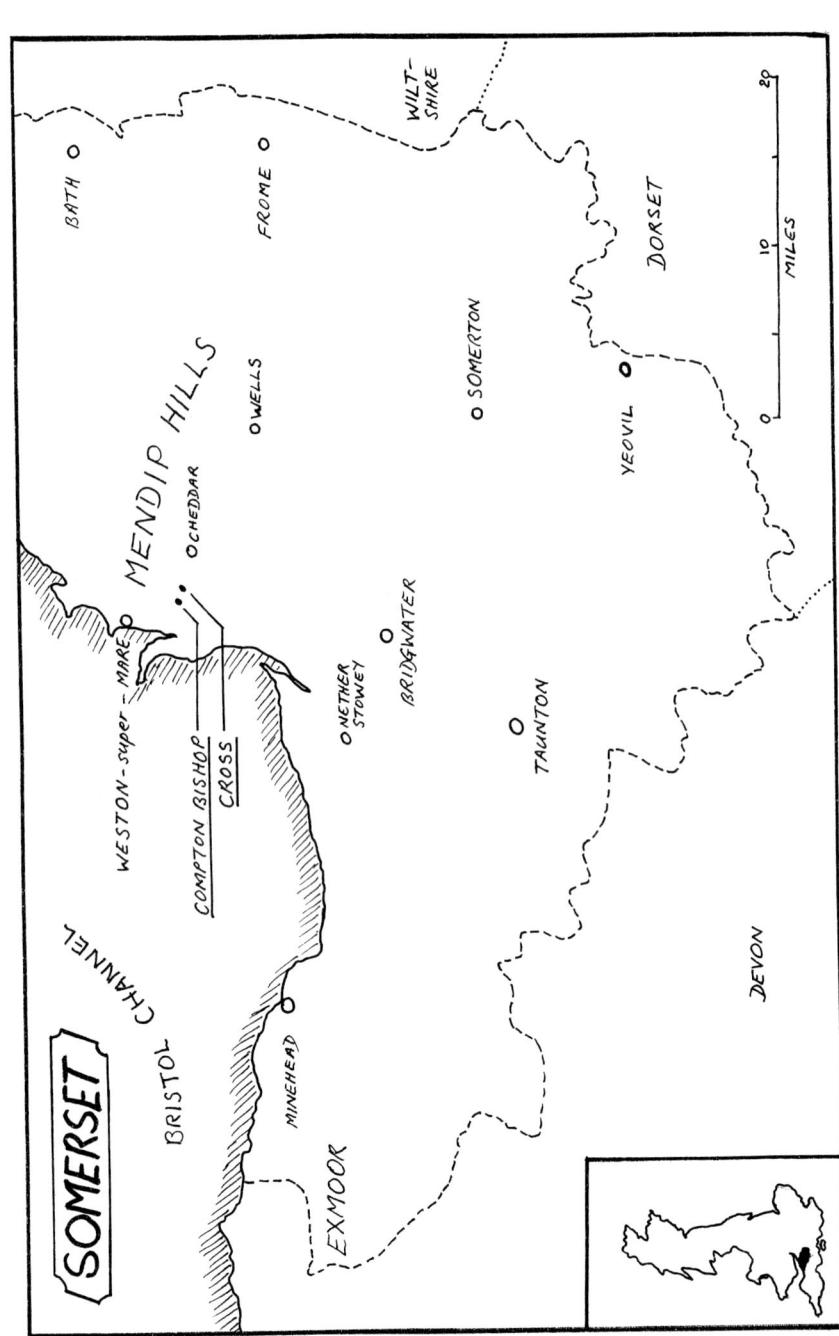

"The contiguous hills of Mendip abound and give grand and extensive prospects"

From a general directory of
the county of Somerset 1846

INTRODUCTION

I have titled this book the story of Compton Bishop and Cross, deliberately avoiding calling it a history of the parish. There are others better qualified than me to write an historical appraisal of our villages, especially when it comes to deciphering ancient documents! I have however sought to be accurate throughout using what information is available together with further knowledge of the times derived from many other sources.

LANDSCAPE AND FEATURES

Compton Bishop (sometimes referred to as Compton Episcopi or Compton Magna) is the name of the ancient manor and later that of the ecclesiastical parish. The area was about three and a half miles long, that is from Loxton to what was the Union Workhouse in Axbridge and about two miles broad. Its irregular outline is determined by natural features although its northern boundary is, for much of its length, the straight Saxon boundary across the top of Wavering Down.

Contained within the old parish (now reduced by boundary changes) are many small groups of houses and farms with names such as Bourton, Webbington (Wiverton or Wibbington), Dunnett (Dunyate) and Rackley (Radcliffe).

Rackley developed as a port after a grant from Richard I to the Bishop of Bath and Wells in 1189. It is said to have been a Roman port from which lead mined at Charterhouse was exported. Experts now feel that this is unlikely as the road across the top of Mendip leads directly to Uphill, a known Roman port. That Rackley was a minor port is not in doubt, coal was imported here from Wales and photographs exist of it being unloaded into "donkey carts directly from the boats by shovel." F. A. Knight mentions a "primitive little quay" with rambling old sheds in which were stored the salt, coal and slate which in former days were brought here from Uphill.

Some twenty five years ago development work around the quay area of Rackley revealed a huge mooring stone set into the bank. The stone measuring five and a half feet by three and a half feet is four and half inches thick and has a circular perforation of approximately eighteen inches with two oblong perforations on either side. It was set deep into the river bank and braced on either side by beams of timber. Through the circular perforation there ran a short loop of chain with an iron ring. The stone was not designed for mooring purposes and it is suggested that it may have been originally a well head. The stone was removed and placed in a cottage garden in Compton Bishop.[1]

The parish of Compton Bishop can be generally divided into two types of terrain; that which is on the southern slope of the Mendips and the moors below. The solid bulk of the hills of Mendip dominate the parish. They have provided grazing and many tenants had the right to turn out sheep on to the hill. An early nineteenth century document of the estate of Walter Long, which included Webbington Farm, mentions the rights "without stint of the tenant" to put eighty to one hundred sheep on the hill from Lady Day to Michaelmas. On the lower slopes the soil is deeper and of excellent quality. It made the area well known for crops of strawberries, peas and early potatoes. This part of Mendip is dominated by Crook Peak and though not particularly high at six hundred and twenty feet it has a conspicuous shape which, from many miles away, can easily be distinguished from other hills in the range. In the days when Britain feared a Spanish invasion (1586 to 1588) Crook Peak was chosen as a beacon hill. The churchwarden's accounts at Banwell contain an entry for expenditure for a load of wood and its carriage to Crook Peak for a beacon.

Burrington Oolite which reaches a thickness of some six hundred feet forms most of the southern slopes of Crook Peak, Compton Hill and Wavering Down. The best example of crags in this are Crook Peak, White Cliff and Yew Tree Cliff. Clifton

Down limestone crops out on the southern lower slope of Crook Peak and in a small area of Cross. The best exposure can be seen in the abandoned quarry in Cross which shows fifty six feet of oolite, dolomite and thin impersistent calcite-mudstones.[2] Curious round stones known as potato stones because of their shape are often found in the area. During the making of the railway cutting and tunnel in 1868 numerous fine specimens were found many containing hollows lined with beautiful crystals. The stone of Mendip has been quarried in the area for hundreds of years. There are several abandoned quarries within the parish which provided stone for building and road making. In 1581 the Crown when leasing the manor to Henry Newton reserved the woods and quarries. No doubt these were the most valuable part of the estate at that time and not surprisingly the monarch chose to keep these in hand. During the 19th century there are accounts for the carriage of "Compton Stone" and gravel to the Mordaunt estate in Warwickshire. There are three caves in the hills above the parish. One in Bourton Coombe was discovered in 1904 by a man quarrying stone. The other two are above Compton Bishop. Fox's Hole and nearby Denny's Hole which when first explored had been, according to a 19th century Kelly's Directory, "splendidly ornamented on the roof and sides with stalactites; but it has unfortunately been rifled."

Stretching away eastwards from Crook Peak is the solid shoulder of Wavering Down the ridge of which is the northern boundary of the parish. This boundary, mentioned in the Saxon Charters, is marked by a stone wall. From Wavering Down the old boundary crosses Shute Shelve, the "Scyte" in the charter. The hills on either side are well wooded. This is a recent development, no doubt caused by lack of management and the decline of grazing. As recently as circa 1925 there are photographs showing the road passing across a moorland like scene. The only recognisable features are the weather beaten Scots Pines. Shute Shelve is said to have been a place of public execution. F. A. Knight notes that Humfry Hawkins and his associates were hanged in irons at Shute Shelve. Travellers must have hurried by this gruesome reminder of "punishment for wicked people." [3]

At the time the Saxon Charter was written the manor boundary of Compton Bishop extended to Axbridge taking in part of what is now West Street. There was a mill close to this eastern boundary of the parish. In The Manorial Court book of 1838 there is an entry stating that the mill, barn and office near Axbridge are "much out of repair". Two fields at this site are called Mill Close. F. A. Knight makes mention of a watermill near Webbington. The parish records of 1737 show the marriage of Robert Crese the millwright, and there are references from time to time of payments made to keep the mill stream clear. The southern boundary is largely defined by the line of the river but as the course of the river has been modified it is difficult to be certain of the old manorial boundary. However ecclesiastical boundaries are often the same as ancient manorial boundaries. By looking at a modern map showing parish boundaries we are probably also looking at both the old manor boundary and the course of the old river Axe.

The Axe and the Cheddar Yeo emerge from under the Mendip hills where relatively high rainfall on the limestone has permeated through to form large streams. In early times these rivers overflowed regularly and along with the inland penetration of tidal waters caused considerable flooding of the low lying areas, particularly in winter. Even in its worst state the area would have provided a livelihood from fish and wildfowl. However, before it could be of use for agriculture it required successful drainage.

Much of this low lying area was in the hands of the great religious houses such as Muchelney, Glastonbury and Wells. Early attempts at water control and drainage were begun by these estates though their technical ability and knowledge at that time achieved only limited success. There were many disputes between Wells and Glastonbury over each others attempts to control water, one side blaming the other for preventing the flow of water, or increasing it and actually flooding pasture!

The straightening of meandering rivers, the widening of rivers and the construction of weirs were being carried out. These were done to prevent or control flooding, to promote the use of a river for trade or provide water for mills. The river Axe appears to have formed part of Compton Bishop manorial boundary and in medieval times it was widened and diverted to flow south of Lower Weare. Two fields behind Riverside Farm (on the edge of Cross but in the parish of Lower Weare) bear the name of Old Port indicating Lower Weare's early history as a river port. (The village was founded circa 1195-1225). Still clearly visible across the field behind Riverside Farm is a ridge of land some three feet high under which are the remains of a medieval road that led from Lower Weare to the river quayside. The Parish boundary continues across the Old Coach Road beside Riverton House and curves away across the fields of Compton Bishop Farm. The river has long since shrunk to become a gently curving rhyne. The river which flows near the western boundary today is known as the Cheddar Yeo. On old maps this river is shown as Little River.

Over many centuries drainage improvements continued. The dissolution of the monasteries meant the distribution of their estates. The Crown became the largest landowner in the area and new stimulus was given to draining activities after the disastrous flood from the sea in 1607. Further impetus came in the mid 18th century as new interest was arising in agriculture. The call for agricultural improvements in Somerset was made by John Billingsley (1747-1811) of Shepton Mallet; it was said of him "He drained Sedgemoor, he enclosed Mendip". Drainage schemes slowly brought hundreds of acres into use for grazing and cultivation.

Before tap water was available most people obtained water from the many springs or wells within the parish. There are several wells that can still be seen in gardens of the old houses. Springs can be found marked in many places on old maps and some of these were exploited in 1898 to form a water supply system. These springs were led into a brick lined well some eight feet by twenty two feet. A brick building was constructed in 1898 to house the well and a steam pump installed to pump the collected water to a reservoir on the hillside above the pumping station. The Kellys Directory of 1902 states that "water is pumped into a reservoir, from this the parishes of Weare, Badgworth, Biddisham, Lympsham, East Brent, Brent Knoll and Mark are supplied". In 1948 a twenty seven horse power Harland Borehole pump was installed capable of pumping 15,000 to 15,300 gallons per hour to a 250 feet head.[4] An interesting footnote to the construction of the pump house in 1898 was the discovery by workmen of a gold bracelet. The bracelet thought to be Bronze Age circa 1400 - 600BC, was designed to be worn on the upper arm and would have been the property of a man of some importance. Was it left as a token of worship to the god of the spring? It is known that valuable items have been left as offerings at wells over the centuries; the custom survives to this day in the form of coins thrown into fountains. The bracelet is now in the British Museum.

The hills above the parish were once part of the ancient forest of Mendip. The term forest describes a hunting ground rather than a wood and in Medieval times it was primarily a place for deer. As a royal forest, Mendip was for the King's deer. A wood was noted in Domesday on the east of Cheddar and Rosewood is probably all that remains of that great wood which covered the hills above Cheddar and Axbridge. King John sold Cheddar to the Bishop of Bath and Wells but retained a wood, perhaps this is the Kings Wood we know today.

Reference is made to three woods in the schedule of the Prowse estate in 1769. Kingswood, just over 12 acres, Polly's wood approximately 6 acres (now part of Kingswood) and Rosewood at 26 acres. Rosewood, now very much larger than it was, is surrounded by secondary woodland. F. A. Knight states that the wood was "planted some 60 years ago and cut every 20 years" but that the southern boundary particularly "bears signs of ancient cultivation" in the form of large ridges that lie east to west. Kingswood today is about the same size as in 1769 and the recent clearing of undergrowth has revealed a great bank set with lime trees that must have been an ancient boundary.

The schedule to value Thomas Prowse's estate in 1769 lists the value of the timber and bark on the home estate and the woods as £311 and the value of the woods as £388. Bark was used for tanning and some of the timber was used on the estate for building or fencing. People can still remember a saw mill opposite Manor Farm, Cross. It contained a saw pit where one man stood deep in the pit and another above the timber pulling a long saw up and down turning felled timber into posts and planks.

The number and beauty of the trees that were in the parish is often commented on. F. A. Knight talks of "the beautiful Spanish chestnut trees outside the northern edge of Kings Wood and the numerous yew trees that may be called a feature of the parish." Knight also mentions the fine elm trees especially south of Compton Bishop village, below Dunnett Farm and Bourton Coombe. Both sides of Cross Lane were also lined with elm trees which contained a huge rookery. Sadly Dutch Elm disease has robbed the area of this particular feature.

In the middle of a field opposite the end of Bourton Lane is a large upright stone of conglomerate some four feet high. Why it is there remains a mystery. Like many standing stones a legend has grown up as to its origins. It is said that the devil hurled the stone from the top of Shute Shelve as part of a contest with a local strong man.

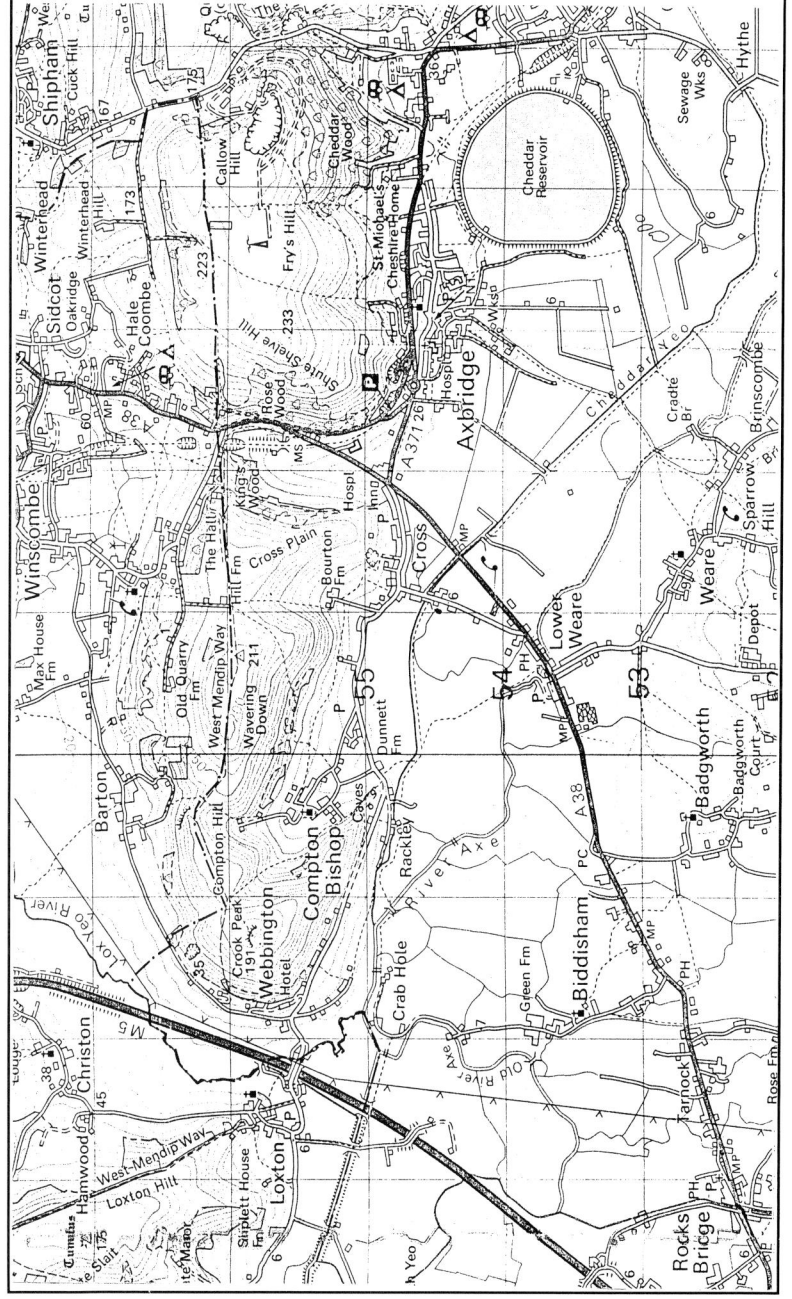

O.S. map of Compton Bishop 1982. Crown copyright.

▲ 1. Aerial view of Cross and Wavering Down.

2. Meandering rhyne behind Riverton House that follows the old parish boundary. ▼

3. The mooring stone now lying in a garden in Compton Bishop. ▶

4. Compton Bishop showing Dunnett Farm. ▼

▲ 5. Wavering Down and Crook Peak.

6. The gold bracelet found in Cross in 1898. ▼

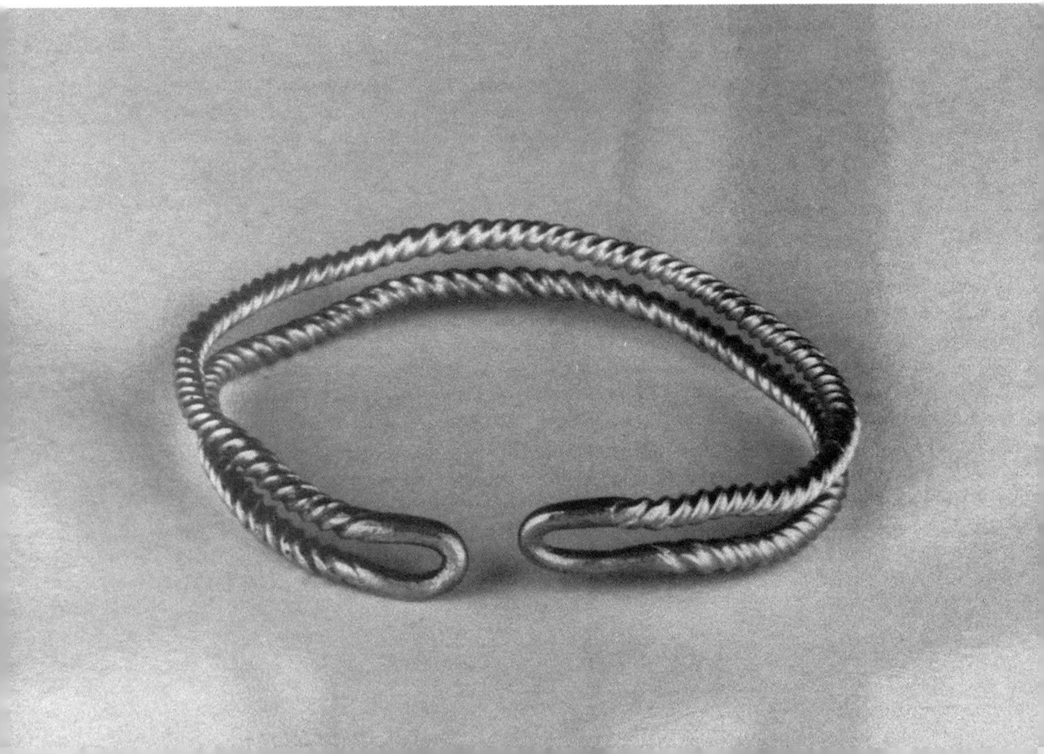

▲ 7. Kingswood. The old boundary bank with its pollarded limes is visible on the right.

8. View of Compton Bishop from Crook Peak. ▼

THE MANOR

Asser, Bishop of Sherborne, writes in his "Life of King Alfred" circa 888 AD that the king sent for him and gave him the gift of two manors, Congresbury and Banwell. In 904 AD Edward the Elder, son of Alfred, obliged Denewulf, Bishop of Winchester to give him three estates in Somerset, Croscombe, Cumbtune and Banwylle in exchange for the "Liberty of Taunton". How Denewulf had acquired Banwell from Sherborne is unclear. It is interesting to note that Cumbtune was shown being worth 10 hides alongside Banwell which was valued at 20 hides. Another charter at the time of Edgar (959-975) mentions the above arrangement but makes Banwell 30 hides with no mention of Compton Bishop. It seems that Compton Bishop was part of Banwell and so it was to remain for many centuries.

Ancient Wessex extended from Surrey to Cornwall and was divided into two bishoprics, Winchester and Sherborne. By the beginning of the tenth century it had become clear that this vast area was too big to be administered by only two bishops and Edward the Elder formed a new see at Wells to which Athelm was consecrated in 909. The crown, now in possession of the manor of Banwell (which included Compton Bishop) appears to have kept it until circa 1033 when King Cnut (1016-1035) gave Banwell and Congresbury to Dudoc the Saxon Bishop of Wells as a personal gift. When Dudoc died in 1060 he bequeathed Congresbury and Banwell to the see of Wells for ever.

Dudoc's successor, Giso, held the manor until Edward the Confessor died in 1066. Harold, hungry for power, at once seized the estates of Congresbury and Banwell as his right as heir to the throne. Giso tried to persuade him, even threatened him with excommunication, but Harold would not give up the manors. Defeated at the Battle of Hastings in 1066 Harold did not live long enough to enjoy what he had taken. William the Conqueror now had possession of Banwell and Congresbury. Bishop Giso returned to pressing his claim for the manors with the new king and within eighteen months the king responded to the pleas and restored the estates to the bishop. The manor was to remain with the see of Wells until 1548 when relationships between the church and the crown were again difficult. The problem began during the reign of Henry VIII when the king failed to persuade the Pope to grant him a divorce from Catherine of Aragon. Many individuals were becoming critical of bishops and envied their rich endowments. It was increasingly argued that the bishops were independent of Parliament and regarded the Pope as their leader. The king wanted the church to be under his complete control and by a series of Acts the links with Rome were gradually severed. Henry VIII appointed himself "supreme head of the church on earth in England" and began appointing bishops. To reduce the bishops powers and defray state costs, bishops were pressurised to grant manors to the Crown. Henry VIII died in 1547. His heir was the 10 year old Prince Edward. Though intelligent this sickly boy was little more than a pawn in the hands of ambitious men such as his uncle the Earl of Hertford. Edward Seymour, Earl of Hertford was waiting in the wings to take power into his own hands before Henry VIII died. He took over the young Edward on his accession and soon had himself made Protector "and governor of his most royal person". He also now had a new title, Duke of Somerset.

The Duke of Somerset was an arrogant man who loved power and money. He built a great palace for himself which he called Somerset House. He began to acquire manors and seemed to be building quite a power base in the west country. Naturally his eyes fell on the manors of the see of Bath and Wells and in a very short time many of these were yielded to the Crown. The manor of Compton Bishop went to the Duke of Somerset. It seems at this time that Compton Bishop was a separate manor from Banwell. Edward, Earl of Warwick was another powerful influence on the young King Edward and by 1549 he was plotting against the Duke of Somerset who now had many enemies. Eventually the Duke of Somerset was to spend time in the Tower of London; he was finally tried for treason and executed on Tower Hill in 1552. The estates he had acquired returned to the Crown. Once more Compton Bishop was a royal manor to be leased out to John Seynt John for 40 years at a yearly rent of £49 3s 9d. Edward VI died in 1553. The young king had actively approved of conversion to Protestant doctrines and during his brief reign he carried forward the reforms enthusiastically started by his father. In 1581 the manor was leased by Elizabeth I to "Henry Newton and Katherine his wife, gentlewomen of the privy chamber" on termination of the lease of John Seynt John "for the service of Katherine". The manor was not a valuable one, particularly as the woods and quarrying were reserved. However, for whatever service Katherine was to provide for the Queen, Henry (later Sir Henry) Newton added Compton Bishop to his holding at Badgworth.

The history of the descent of the manor becomes a little vague at this point. The will, dated 1667, of William Prowse leaves "to my cosen (sic) John Prowse - all my manors of Compton Magna, and Badgworth". The will shows William Prowse had land at Weare, Wedmore, Biddisham, Mark,

South Brent, Lympsham, Weston-super-Mare, Winscombe, Banwell, Congresbury, Wick St. Lawrence, Portishead, Nympet, Wells, Wookey, Spaxton, Cannington, Stogursey, and Fiddington. So who was William Prowse and how did he come into possession of the manor of Compton Bishop?

The memorial to William Prowse (1590-1670) in Axbridge Church gives some clues to the man. It says he was a lawyer "skilled if anyone ever was" and that he came from a notable family. The memorial is very large, dominating the end wall of the north aisle. It shows a man in clothes of a severely plain style. The face has been well modelled suggesting it was made to be a good likeness. There is no mention of his wife on his memorial. He had married Frances Jeffreys (1617-1666) of Axbridge in 1645 when he was 55 years old (Frances was the daughter of James Jeffreys, Mayor of Axbridge).

William Prowse was part of a family so profuse that it could be found all over Devon and Somerset; so large in fact that they are sometimes difficult to trace with certainty. The Prowse family claim to have come over with the Conqueror and almost certainly this is true. They are thought to be descended from Eudo de Prouz or Preaux on whom was bestowed the Manor of Gidley as Warden of Dartmoor. By the 13th century the family was firmly established in Chagford (Devon) and many had become lawyers, merchants and landowners. They appear to have had the knack of making advantageous marriages, acquiring property in many places although seeming to remain a largely West Country family.

It is not clear how William Prowse acquired the manor of Compton Bishop. In his own book of lands purchased, dated 1644, he notes that in 1641 the Manor was held jointly by William Caple and William Edwards later between William Edwards and William Prowse. By 1652 Prowse himself was lord of the manor. Clearly parts of the manor had been broken up and sold and from as early as 1644 William Prowse had been purchasing land "to join to the manor again". It may be that William inherited the manor. It is more likely that William Prowse purchased the manor of Compton Bishop just as in 1630 he had purchased the Manor of Badgworth from John Newton at a cost of £1630.

By 1670 John Prowse, a country gentleman, was possessed of the manor. Even here there is some confusion as the memorial in Axbridge church says that John Prowse was nephew and heir of William Prowse. William's will however leaves his manor "to my Cosen (sic) John Prowse". Perhaps the memorial was wrongly inscribed! It is known that John Prowse married Anna Spearing daughter of William Spearing. William Spearing who was four times mayor of Axbridge was a brother-in-law of William Prowse having married William's sister Agnes. (It was William Spearing that left the bread legacy which is still fulfilled every week when bread is placed in a glass fronted cupboard in Axbridge church). Anna Prowse died in 1668 at the age of twenty three. Her memorial, also in Axbridge church, shows a pious kneeling figure surrounded by fat cherubs on which she is described as "virtuous, of a radiant nature and sincere innocence".

John Prowse remarried in 1670. His second wife was Anne Newborough, daughter and co-heiress of Roger Newborough of Berkley (near Frome) adding the estate of Berkley to the Prowse family. They had seven children and it was their second son also called John who was to succeed to the manor.

John, born 1676, married Margaret Bragge in 1701. She died the following year in childbirth. She is buried with her stillborn daughter at Compton Bishop. A large marble monument inside Compton Bishop church above the pulpit is a memorial to his first wife, his parents and his three brothers and three sisters.

In 1706 John Prowse remarried. His new wife was Abigail Hooper daughter of George Hooper, Bishop of Bath and Wells. Abigail was said to be of "agreeable manners and eminent piety". She was a considerable benefactress to the church in Axbridge to which she gave many items including an altar piece, a table and a cloth which she embroidered herself. The cloth took seven years to complete and can be seen displayed in Axbridge church. To Compton Bishop church she gave a silver cup in 1763. John Prowse was a Justice of the Peace, Colonel of the Bath Regiment and a Knight of the Shire. He was called to Parliament in 1708. Unfortunately he fell victim to smallpox and died at Westminster in 1710 when only thirty three years old. The care and management of the estate and upbringing of their only child, three year old Thomas, fell to Abigail. We can see from the inscription on her memorial that she dedicated the early part of her life to the care and education of her son. In 1730 Abigail turned her energies to rebuilding, with great care, the house at Berkley which was to be her home until her death in 1763. Perhaps it was at this time that Thomas Prowse developed an interest in architecture. The house remained in the hands of the Prowse family until 1800 when it passed to the Mordaunt family until it was sold in 1919. In 1731 Thomas, aged 25, married Elizabeth Sharp. Elizabeth was daughter and co-heiress of John Sharp, Grafton Park in Northamptonshire, bringing the estate of Grafton and Wicken to the Prowse family. Thomas and Elizabeth had eight children five of whom died young. The three surviving were George, Mary and Elizabeth. Thomas Prowse was Sheriff of Somerset and a member of Parliament from 1740. Horace Walpole described him as "the most knowing and the most moderate of Tories". By 1761 his name was being suggested as Speaker of the House which seemed to have been a popular choice. However Prowse refused for "fear of impairing my health" which was already causing some concern.

Like many country gentlemen of the time Thomas Prowse had an interest in the arts, particularly architecture. He assisted his friend Sanderson Miller, who clearly had great respect for his opinions, in his architectural designs for Hagley Hall, Worcestershire and Shire Hall in Warwick. He executed his own designs at Hatch Court (Hatch Beauchamp, Somerset) and Wicken Church (Northamptonshire) and he is also credited with the designs for Berkley Church (near Frome),and alterations for Kimberley Hall (Norfolk). A poem written about Kimberley Hall contains the following lines "fix'd by Prowse's just Palladian hand, its towered honour stands".

Thomas Prowse died in 1767 and his widow went to live at Berkley House. He was succeeded by his son George (born 1737). George Prowse had married Elizabeth Sharp, daughter of Dr. Thomas Sharp, Archdeacon of Northamptonshire, in 1762. They had been living on the Northamptonshire part of the Prowse estate when, within a few months of his fathers death, George Prowse died at the age of thirty. George Prowse had no heir so the estate of Thomas Prowse was divided between his surviving daughters Mary and Elizabeth. A schedule attached to the Act of Separation gives a complete guide to the Prowse estate and how it was to be divided. In addition to the manor of Compton Bishop, Berkley, Badgworth and Weare there was land or property in several counties including Worcestershire, Wiltshire, Dorset and the City of London. There were houses, land or farms at Nympnet, Wick St. Lawrence, Priddy, Cannington, Bishops Lydeard and the City of Wells.

The Northamptonshire estate remained with George Prowse's widow Elizabeth until her death in 1810 when it reverted to Elizabeth Mordaunt (nee Prowse) by then the only remaining Prowse heiress. Mary Prowse (1745-1800) received the manor of Berkley and later Rodden and Fulbrook (Wiltshire). In 1783 she married John Methuen, Rector of Berkley. They had no surviving children.

Elizabeth Prowse (1749-1826) received the manors of Badgworth, Weare and Compton Bishop. In 1769 she married John Mordaunt bringing with her a considerable dowry, her portion of the estate of Thomas Prowse being worth nearly £36,000. John Mordaunt's father, Sir Charles Mordaunt and Thomas Prowse were long standing friends and had much in common, both having served in Parliament. The Mordaunts were also an old family proud to trace their ancestors back to the time of William the Conqueror. The manor was now in the hands of the Mordaunts of Walton Hall in Warwickshire where it was to remain until the mid twentieth century. Within a year of her wedding Elizabeth gave birth "with gratifying ease" to a daughter, to be followed by seven more children before 1780. The children often spent the summer with their grandmother Elizabeth Prowse at Berkley House in Somerset.

Sir John Mordaunt died in 1806 and was succeeded by his second child Charles who was also to become a Member of Parliament although poor health made him a frequent absentee from the House. He married his childhood friend Marianne Holbech in 1807 and they had three children. Charles Mordaunt spent a considerable amount of time and money improving Walton Hall and its estate. He died in 1823. His son John continued to encourage improved farming on the estate. He lived in some style with ample staff, good horses and smart carriages. He was however generous to the labouring poor and created allotments for them with prizes for the best kept garden. Many worthy causes had his support. He was an exceptionally conscientious Member of

Parliament and very well informed. He had married Caroline Sophia Murrey in 1834 and they had four children. An unfortunate shooting accident led to his early death at the age of 37.

John's son (yet another Charles) tenth Baronet, travelled much in Europe; he entered Parliament at the youthful age of twenty three. Charles married the beautiful Harriet Moncrieff who spent a lot of time enjoying London society. She became friendly with the Prince of Wales (later Edward VII) and rumours were rife. Everyone knew the Prince visited her at her London house. When Harriet had a daughter, Violet in 1869, Sir Charles became convinced that the child was not his and he embarked on a divorce that shocked society. The Prince of Wales was called to the witness box but Sir Charles was unable to procure a divorce.

A story is told (and it certainly found its way into talk in Compton Bishop) that Sir Charles returned home from a fishing trip to find the Prince of Wales leaning on his doorway smoking a cigar watching Lady Mordaunt driving a little cart drawn by two white ponies that the Prince of Wales had given her. Sir Charles was so angered by the scene that he produced a gun and shot both ponies dead. He later obtained a divorce citing Lord Cole. He eventually found happiness with his second wife Mary (nee Cholmondley) and their six children. Sir Charles died in 1897. [5]

The Manor of Compton Bishop remained with the Mordaunts of Walton Hall, Warwickshire until the second half of this century.

▲ 9. William Prowse memorial in Axbridge Church.

▲ 10. Thomas Prowse, thought to be by Thomas Gainsborough.

11. Elizabeth Prowse, wife of Thomas Prowse, thought to be by Thomas Gainsborough. ▼

12. Elizabeth Mordaunt (nee Prowse) by Thomas Hudson. ▼

▲ 13. Anna Prowse memorial in Axbridge Church.

14. Hatch Court near Taunton, designed by Thomas Prowse. ▼

THE COACH ROAD

An old directory of Somerset (dated 1859) describes Cross as "a small village containing three respectable posting houses. It is not remarkable for anything, but most of the coaches both up and down to Plymouth and Exeter change horses here" . No doubt from earliest times many people living in the village earned their living from travellers using the old road from Bristol to Exeter and Plymouth. The story of that road is, in large measure, the story of Cross.

  The Romans left Briton with many miles of hard wearing roads. By the Middle Ages these were becoming neglected or had disappeared altogether. Pack horses carried goods over long distances on roads that were unfit most of the year for wheeled transport. People travelled on horseback and only those unable to ride used a carriage or cart. The first attempt at improving the country's roads was the Highways Act of 1555. This Act provided there should be a highways surveyor in each parish and that every person holding land over a certain value should supply labour or tools for work on the parish highway. The Act failed to set a standard of maintenance and was difficult to enforce so that standards varied from parish to parish. Nevertheless it remained the only attempt at road improvement for nearly three hundred years and almost all roads in England were in a very bad state especially in winter. By the eighteenth century there arose a need to create better roads to improve trade. Private enterprise stepped in and Turnpike Trusts were set up by Acts of Parliament. Trusts constructed roads or improved existing highways and collected fees from road users in return for maintaining the road. The road from Bristol to Bridgwater (now the A38) was a turnpike road administered by the Bristol Trust set up in 1726. John MacAdam became General Surveyor of roads in Bristol in 1816. The Bristol Trust had in its care the road from Bristol to Exeter as far south as Brent Knoll.

Milestones that guided travellers to their destination were fitted with iron plates marking the distance between towns. (These were later replaced by iron posts). An old milestone can be found on the left side of the A38 going up Shute Shelve almost opposite the entrance to the Arbour Nursing Home. The iron plate is missing but the fixing holes can still be seen. The post that once stood in the village of Cross has now been resited on the A38. Like many other mileposts that survive beside the modern A38 the distance to Cross is shown indicating how important Cross was to travellers who often must have been relieved to be nearing the warmth and shelter of the village inns.

A series of gates were set up at intervals along turnpike roads. Houses were constructed for gatekeepers who collected the tolls before opening the gate to let the traveller through. A typical tollhouse was semi circular with a porch to keep the gateman dry in wet weather. By the gate or fixed to the house was a board stating the charges for different types of road users. There was a gate and gatekeepers cottage in Cross where the Old Coach Road makes a left turn towards Lower Weare. The gatekeepers cottage was on the site now occupied by Cross memorial hall. The 1861 census is the last recorded evidence of Cross Gate when the house was occupied by the gatekeeper Henry Carter, his wife and three children.

Cross Gate and the gate at Sidcot went before living memory but the tollhouse at Churchill was not demolished until the early 1960's. A photograph shows it to have been a two storey house with a veranda. At Churchill the coach road ran steeply up hill beside the Crown Inn (this part of the road fell into disuse when the section of road passing Dolebury Camp was constructed in the 1820's). The remains of the old road can be seen today being used regularly by riders and walkers between the Crown Inn and the Star Inn.

As roads improved people began to travel about more. For those not wealthy enough to own a private coach the only form of travel was to hire a chaise. These carriages were driven from a box seat or more usually by a man, known as a postillion, riding the nearside horse. Post Chaises could cover the ground at a spanking pace, sending up clouds of dust in the summer and covering the postillion with mud in the winter. They were often owned by innkeepers who hired them out complete with horses and postillions.

There were three inns in Cross often referred to in old directories as posting houses. The Kings Arms is now Manor Farm and situated at the foot of Shute Shelve Hill. In a book listing land and property that he purchased William Prowse notes that he acquired the Kings Arms Inn in 1681 for £105.

The New Inn has been found recorded in a deed dated as early as 1665. The White Hart Inn is almost certainly of a similar date. Unfortunately the only evidence that has come to light so far is a Land Tax Assessment of 1821 which shows that Richard Dell was at that time the owner of The White Hart Inn. In 1827 it was rented for 5/- p.a. to George Bees. In 1852 it was purchased by the Mordaunt family for £200.

The White Hart and The New Inn remain inns to this day. They had a chaise house attached and were presumably hiring out post chaises. In the early 1800's there are several records of men in the parish including John Taylor, Abraham Millard, James Tucker and Thomas Collard who give their occupation as chaise driver.

At various times both The New Inn and The White Hart have made claims to be the site of the infamous Judge Jeffreys Bloody Assizes. The large rooms at both The White Hart and The New Inn are said to have been the court in which the Assize was held. More likely they are the rooms in which, at various times, the Manor Court met. After the Battle of Sedgemoor when the Duke of Monmouth's rebellion was finally crushed the King appointed Lord Chief Justice Jeffreys to bring the rebels to trial. Sentences handed out were intended to strike fear across the countryside. The lucky ones were transported. Those sentenced to death were hung drawn and quartered and the gruesome remains left at gallows for all to see. The nearest town where Judge Jeffreys held his Assize was Wells.

The coach road was said to have brought famous people to Cross. There are stories that Queen Victoria travelled through the village on her way to Exeter. Another says she stayed overnight at the Kings Arms Inn. Sadly this does not appear to be the case. The Royal Archives at Windsor Castle are emphatic that Queen Victoria never stayed at Cross. They add "The Queen kept a detailed diary throughout her life and the only occasion on which she mentions travelling through Somerset was on 15th August 1856 when she travelled by train from Devonport through Taunton and Exeter to Bristol." [6]

Charles Dickens is said to have modelled Miss Havisham, a character in his novel Great Expectations, on a lady who lived at Newton House in Cross. It is quite common for a community to produce a person with eccentric or mysterious behaviour about whom stories are woven. It is impossible to be certain which resident, if any, of Newton House caused these rumours to start. The most likely candidate must be Miss Carde who was living at Newton House in 1861. It is interesting to note that the census of 1871 and 1881 shows Newton House to be uninhabited although the Kelly's Directories continue to list Miss Carde as a resident of Cross until 1880. In the 1861 census Mary Carde gave her age as 45 and stated that she was born in Mark. There is no baptism recorded for Mary Carde in Mark parish register but it does contain the baptisms of eight children of John Carde, gentleman, between 1817 and 1822. There is a tombstone in Mark churchyard listing several members of the Carde family including a Mary who died aged 86 in 1901.

It would not be difficult to weave a story about a middle aged woman who, it seems, lived alone at Newton House in 1861. Add to this the picture of Newton House uninhabited for considerable lengths of time, the shutters closed, no lights at night and we have the makings of a fine story to tell around the fireside. Many claims have been made for models for Miss Havisham. The most likely candidate is Martha Joachim. A journal, which Dickens edited, carried details of an inquest in 1850 into the death of "a wealthy and eccentric lady" who died in Marylebone in London. Several tragic events in her life had turned Miss Joachim into a recluse who dressed all in white.

David Parker, Curator of the Dickens House Museum in London said in 1988 "While it is impossible to prove or refute any case, in the absence of Dickens having said who his model was, if any, I have to say the lady at Newton House in Cross seems an unlikely candidate."[7] The evidence that Queen Victoria or Charles Dickens stayed or even passed through Cross is therefore doubtful. However, the village did have at least three famous guests.

Samuel Coleridge the poet lived in the Quantock Hills at Nether Stowey, Somerset, and made numerous journeys, often on foot, between there and Bristol. In 1797 Coleridge's friend William Wordsworth and his sister Dorothy came to live quite close by at Alfoxden and all three regularly explored the surrounding countryside. In May 1798 Dorothy and William Wordsworth and Samuel Coleridge walked from Stowey to Cheddar, a distance of some thirty miles. We know from the letters written by Coleridge whilst in Cross and from the brief notes in Dorothy's journal that whilst on the walk they stayed overnight at Cross. [8]

John MacAdam was also a visitor to Cross. According to John Bowen of Bridgwater MacAdam stayed in Cross whilst gathering information on road making techniques. John Loudon MacAdam (1756-1836) had travelled widely to ascertain the best means of road making. He soon realised that there was a need for strong solid surfaces "over which carriages may pass without any impediment."

MacAdam's visit to Cross may have been to meet with Gabriel Stone (circa 1754-1815) of Somerset Farm, Brent Knoll who claimed the credit for introducing a road so smooth that coachmen complained it made them careless. Certainly MacAdam was to cite a stretch of "excellent road near to Bridgewater(sic) where stone was well broken" as one of the roads that influenced his ideas for a technique of road construction that was to put a new word into the English language. As early as 1824 The Times newspaper was reporting that a stretch of road from Charing Cross in London had been MacAdamised.

Unfortunately it is impossible to say which of the inns in Cross hosted these famous travellers.

The development of an enormous coaching network that was to cover most of the country was brought about by improved roads and improved vehicles. Early coaches had a rounded roof and passengers sat only inside. They used the same horses from the start to the finish of a journey ridden by postillions. As business increased more money was invested in improved coaches, relays of horses were set up along the route and speeds increased. Better coach designs allowed for passengers on the roof and beside the driver who was now sitting on a box seat on top of the coach. Later coaches could take fourteen to sixteen passengers with the majority travelling outside.

Coach masters set up routes using inns as places to change horses and provide rest and refreshment for passengers. The three inns in Cross were all involved in the coaching trade on the turnpike road. The position of the village, approximately twenty miles from Bristol, afforded an ideal place to change horses replacing those travelling south that had just hauled the coach up over Mendip and setting in a new team for the north bound coach's pull up Shute Shelve Hill.

The working life of a coach horse was hard and short; on average three years. To "die in harness" was an expression coined in the great days of coaching. Horsing a coach was the most expensive and difficult part of running a coach route and many horses were required to service each route. Even the largest operator running a network of coach routes was at the mercy of the innkeepers on their routes to supply good quality animals. The Kings Arms (now Manor Farm) appears to be the only one of the inns in Cross to have had a separate business for horsing the coaches. In 1851 the innkeeper was John Burdge and James Millard was grazier and stablekeeper of the Kings Arms stable.

Inns provided hospitality and shelter to travellers for centuries. Local inns were a meeting place for farmers, dealers, packmen and drovers. Inn keepers often enjoyed a high status in the community. Inns often issued a coin-like token known as a check. The origin of public house checks is obscure but their use was widespread from the 1850's to the end of the century."[9] There is a check made of brass with a milled edge in the Leicester Museum. Its value of 1½d is stamped on one side and on the reverse side is 'The White Hart Hotel, Cross'. The inn parlour was the news centre of the village, not only for local gossip but for news from beyond the parish brought in by travellers. Innkeepers were expected to be able to provide food and drink for weary travellers at any hour of the day or night. Thomas Hughes in his book Tom Brown's Schooldays, describes a stop for breakfast, a scene that would have been familiar in any coaching inn including those in Cross:

> "There in the low, dark wainscoted room hung with sporting prints - the table covered with the whitest of cloths and china and bearing a pigeon pie, ham, round of cold boiled beef and a great loaf of household bread on a wooden trencher. And in comes a stout headwaiter, puffing under a tray of hot viands, kidney and steak, transparent rashers and poached eggs, buttered toast and muffins, coffee and tea all smoking hot." [10]

It is difficult to imagine today's quiet village of Cross busy with travellers and noisy with the business of preparing the coaches and horses for the next leg of a journey. A stop to change horses would draw a crowd of admirers and many coach drivers became local heroes. In the early days of coaching, drivers were notorious for being rough, coarse men with red faces. Frequent stops at inns where they seldom had to buy their own food or drink gave them a drunken reputation. But all this was to change in the nineteenth century when faster coaches running to demanding timetables required better coachmen who became figures of considerable elegance who managed their teams of horses with considerable skill.

Despite better roads, better coaches and increased driving skills, travelling by coach was uncomfortable, especially for those travelling outside, and often dangerous. The time of arrival stated on coach company advertisements was often followed by the words IF GOD PERMIT. The safe completion of a journey so often depended on favourable roads and weather. Common hazards faced by coach travellers were flooded roads, ice and snow, overturning coaches, horses bolting and harnesses breaking. The Reverend Arthur Powell writing in 1908 recounts that a friend told him "My grandfather journeyed once to London and back and he was careful, at the advice of his lawyer, to make his will before he went. He also had a hot bath on the night before he set out so that in the event of an accident as he said, he might make a clean corpse."[11] Going downhill was a particularly tricky procedure. A wise coachman would pull up his horses and inspect the harness before descending a hill. No doubt Shute Shelve required these precautions before the weary team met the challenge of the long descent to the inns at Cross where fresh horses would be waiting.

Footpads and highwaymen were always a possible danger to travellers. It was not until the nineteenth century that highway robbery became a rare occurrence. Penalties for captured highwaymen were barbaric; often they were hung from a gibbet for all to see. In Chew Magna churchyard there is a tombstone to a William Fowler who was "shot by a highwayman on Dundry Hill in 1814". In Congresbury a Charles Capell Hardwick, who died in 1848 who "was of such courage that, being attacked by a highwayman on the heath of this parish on 20th October 1830, and fearfully wounded by him, he pursued his assailant and, having overtaken him in the centre of the village, delivered him to Justice". Although there is no record of the apprehension of a highwayman on the old coach road the journey over Mendip would surely have provided plenty of hiding places and opportunity for would be villains.

By the end of the eighteenth century the improved performance of the stage coaches put pressure on the Post Office to improve their delivery of mail. Although it was against the law to send letters other than by the post office, people began to disguise letters as parcels so that they could travel on a fast coach thereby defrauding the post office of its revenue. Previously mail had been carried by Post boys (these were in fact men not boys) riding on horseback. They delivered to post houses, which were denoted by a post horn sign above the door, where recipients went to collect their mail.

John Palmer, son of a Bath merchant, put forward a plan to run special high speed coaches on a strict schedule. These would have been run by contractors and carried an armed guard to protect the mail. The first mail coach ran between Bristol and London in August 1784. The journey took seventeen hours, previously the post had taken up to three days. Within a short time mail coaches became a popular way to travel even though they were more expensive.

Standard mail coaches were built by John Vidler of London. They were decorated in maroon and black with scarlet wheels and had a royal coat of arms on the door panels. The guard in charge of the mailbags wore a scarlet livery and was armed with a blunderbuss and pistols. He sat with the mailbags in a special locker under his feet. When the mail coach came in sight of a toll house (the mail coach was exempt from toll charges) he took out a horn from beside his seat and with a resounding flourish let the gatekeeper know to fling open the gate to allow the mail through; a sight and sound that must have been familiar to people in Cross when the toll house was manned (see page 24). With the introduction of mail coaches post boys were gradually made redundant as letter carriers and often became postillions or chaise drivers (See page 25).

As with stage-coaches the horses for the mail coaches were supplied by contractors along the route. The Post Office allowed only five minutes to change horses. Any time lost had to be made up on the next stage as precise timekeeping was essential. The mail coaches were so punctual that villagers along the route set their clocks and watches by them.

People were proud of "their" mail coach and would often gather to see it arrive and depart. The coach and its driver were often heroes to small boys and, on celebrations such as Christmas, would decorate their coach, the horses, the guard and the coachman with festoons and ribbons. The following list from the Piggots Directory of 1830 shows the names of some of the coaches calling at Cross at that time and gives an impression of a high level of activity.

Bristol to Bridgewater *Duke of Wellington*
   Calls at The White Hart Inn every Tuesday, Thursday and Saturday at 12.30pm
Bristol to Barnstable *Royal Mail*
   Calls at the Kings Arms every morning at a quarter before 12
Exeter to Birmingham *The Times*
   Kings Arms every afternoon at 2.30pm
Exeter to Birmingham *Duke of Wellington*
   The White Hart - Monday, Wednesday, Thursday at 12.30pm
Bristol to Exeter *The Times*
   The Kings Arms every morning at 10.00

33

Bristol to Exeter   *The Comet*
  The White Hart - Monday, Wednesday and Friday at 12.30pm
Bristol to Exeter   *Estafette* (mail)
  Kings Arms daily at 12.30pm
Bristol to Plymouth   *Non Pariel*
  The White Hart daily (ex Sunday) 9.00am and 7.00pm
Cheltenham to Exeter   *Exquisite*
  The Kings Arms daily (ex Sunday) 2.30pm
Bristol to Plymouth   *Exonian* (mail)
  Kings Arms daily 9.00am returns 4.00pm
Taunton to Bristol   *John O'Groats*
  The White Hart every day (ex Sunday) at 11.00am

From this list it appears that The New Inn was no longer serving as a coaching inn by 1830 although it may have still have been serving local routes such as Wells to Weston-super-Mare.

The so called Golden Age of coaching was brief lasting only fifty years or so. The coming of the railway meant the coach routes that competed with the railways were to disappear almost overnight. Coaches that operated on minor routes survived for longer but eventually branch lines made even these redundant. As coaching declined inns suffered badly from loss of trade. Some were sold and became private houses. This was to be the fate of the King's Arms which had ceased trading as an inn by 1861 and became a farm. Some inns managed to retain a modest trade from local coach routes. A coach called "The Star" which ran from Wells to Yatton continued to call at The New Inn. Other inns closed rooms no longer required and became public houses for local trade. The 1830 Tithe map shows that The White Hart Inn occupied, with the exception of the smith's shop, the site now occupied by the terrace of cottages on the east side of the inn. This part of the building no longer required by the inn was divided into the cottages that can be seen today.

In 1894 The White Hart described itself in directories as a hotel and had established itself as the venue for a completely different form of traveller - the cyclist. The advent of the "safety bicycle" in 1887 led to cycling becoming a craze with both sexes. On summer days thousands left towns and cities to enjoy the countryside encouraged by the formation of cycling clubs. One of these, the Cyclists' Touring Club (CTC), which at its peak had over sixty thousand members, had a headquarters at The White Hart which was pleased to announce that it offered "accommodation for cyclists and pleasure parties".

Local horse drawn traffic was little affected by the railways. In some cases it may have increased as carriers transported goods to and from newly opened stations. However Cross's days in the story of coach travel were drawing to a close. Hunt's directory of 1850 says of Cross "it formerly appeared more bustling than at present, no doubt in some measure owing to the passing of mail and stage coaches - but by the opening of the Bristol - Exeter railway these vehicles have become entirely annihilated; and the smiling Jehu, the cracking whip, the rattling wheels, the prancing horses and the sound of the horn, no longer enlivens the village".

▲ 15. Turnpike marker near Brent Knoll. A turnpike milestone showing 6 miles to Cross and 10 miles to Bridgwater.

▲ 16. The Toll House at Horsington, Somerset.

◄ 17. Part of the old coach road near The Crown at Churchill.

18. Manor Farm at Cross formerly The Kings Arms. ▼

▲ 19. The New Inn, Cross. Note the Starkey, Knight and Ford sign on the end wall.

20. The road from Shute Shelve hill circa 1925, now the A38. ▼

▲ 21. The White Hart Inn, Cross.

▼ 22. Two sides of a Pub token issued by The White Hart Hotel (Inn). ▼

▲ 23. Cross, showing Moorland Farm and the White Hart.

24. Manor Farm, Compton Bishop. ▼

COMMUNITY LIFE

Evidence of early settlements on Mendip are uncovered from time to time when weapons, flint axe heads and arrow tips are found.

Early man lived in caves on Mendip and there are several caves within the parish. They hunted wild animals and on the waterlogged levels found fish, eels and wildfowl. How long there have been settlements at Compton Bishop and Cross is uncertain. The "ton" ending the name of Compton suggests Saxon origins - the name meaning the ton (or settlement) in the Coombe. Later the name became Compton Episcopi denoting the bishop's ownership, later still Compton Magna whilst the manor was in the hands of the Crown. William Prowse's seventeenth century will refers only to his manor at Compton.

The village of Cross does not appear on early maps such as Saxtons map to Somerset dated 1575. This may be because it was not considered important enough to mention. A Feet of Fine in the reign of Henry V(1413-1422) mentions Compton, Crosse, (Sic) Overwere and Nytherwere. Early references indicate that the village of Cross was centred at the base of Shute Shelve hill where the road turned right in front of the New Inn. (The new road, now the A38 was not put through until the 1930's). The village had no doubt earned a living from travellers who stopped to rest their horses before climbing the hill long before the age of coaching. The name Cross, it has been suggested, was because it was at a cross road. This seems unlikely as the cross road is modern. That it was the site of a religious cross seems a more likely explanation. In a deed dated 1773 the bounds of the manor are described thus:- "That the bounds of the said manor of Compton Bishop begin at a Cross anciently made before any of our memorys" (sic).

Christianity came early to the West Country and Aldhelm was made Bishop of the West Saxons in 705 AD. Celtic saints are associated with many Somerset churches. There is legend that St. Congar founded a bishopric of Somerset at Congresbury. (The only dedication to St. Congar in England is Badgworth church). Legend also tells how Christianity came to Somerset when Joseph of Arimathea came to south west England and established a community of monks at Glastonbury. The abbey at Glastonbury, and later the bishops of Wells, were to have a considerable influence on the development of Compton Bishop and Cross for many centuries.

The beautiful and ancient church at Compton Bishop is the most obvious link with the past. Dedicated to St. Andrew it was consecrated by Bishop Jocelin in 1236. The bishop gifted "ten acres in his moor of Cumtun to enclose with a dyke, and licence to pasture ten oxen with the oxen of the bishop in his manor of Cumtun."[12] In the churchyard, along with the old Yew tree, is an ancient cross that once had six steps below the shaft but now only has four. In 1847 the Reverend E. Fleming-Bleadon had, at his own expense, a stone cross put on top of the shaft but this was later removed.

There are no very old tombstones in the churchyard, those still readable in the chancel floor date from 1690. The corner of the churchyard at one time contained a poor house. The Overseer of the Poor's account book in the early nineteenth century notes the expenditure of three shillings and sixpence for "hauling a family's goods to the poor house" and expenditure on lime to paint the poor house.

The design of the church tower is linked by Peter Poyntz Wright in his book The Parish Churches of Somerset to those of Compton Martin, Kewstoke and Churchill. He describes the tower as early Perpendicular architecture and dates it at circa 1380. The tower was damaged in the Great Storm of November 1703 when a gale which lasted two days did considerable damage. This same storm swept away the Eddystone lighthouse and killed Bishop Kidder and his wife in the Bishop's Palace at Wells when a chimney stack collapsed. The account books at Compton Bishop show the expenditure of three pounds seventeen shillings and sixpence in 1705 to John Logtory "ye mason for thirty one days work in mending the church tower". In the eighteenth century sparrows appear to have been a problem within the church. The account book shows a payment of three pence a dozen for sparrows (killed or trapped). In 1723 it amounted to thirty nine dozen birds. One wonders why the birds were such a problem, perhaps the windows were not fully glazed. Inside the tower are six bells two of which are inscribed "W. W. Bilbie 1711", and two "Mr. John Fry and William Wickham - churchwardens 1773 - A. Bilbie". The Fry family name appears over many generations in Compton Bishop and Axbridge; later the family were residents at Compton House, Axbridge. The Wickhams lived for many generations at Manor Farm, Compton Bishop and were described by John Rutter in 1828 as "the once wealthy and respectable family of Wickham". The Bilbies were a family of bell founders of Chew Stoke whose name appears on many Mendip church bells including Loxton, Axbridge and Winscombe.

On the north wall of the chancel is a memorial for several members of the Henning family. Robert Henning purchased the Rectory of Compton Bishop from William Mycombe. Henning was a naval man and the family connections with the sea continued through his son Hamilton who became a navy surgeon and through his daughter who married a Royal Naval commander William Martin in Compton Bishop church in 1816. Robert Henning and his wife Margaret had twelve children, seven of whom appear on the memorial stone. They lived at the Rectory which had at one time been the Parsonage. The Parsonage is described in a Compton Bishop church Terrier dated 1674 as having a "hall, Parlour, Kitchen, Buttery and several lodging chambers". It was "built of stone with slatt (sic). One court before, one orchard, one stone barn and a pasture adjoining". The house was rebuilt, according to F. A. Knight, by Henning some time before 1823 using materials of the older rectory. This site is now occupied by Compton House, Compton Bishop.

In the early years of this century the entries in Compton Bishop parish registers serve as a record of births, marriages and deaths but, especially in the eighteenth century, the register often includes comments by the vicar that tell us something of the community in which he had the care of souls. There are notes on anyone who died of smallpox. No doubt this was to prevent the grave being disturbed at a later date because smallpox remains active in a grave for many years. In 1754 when Mary Emory died of smallpox the vicar notes she was the servant of Mr. Partridge. One can easily imagine the consternation in the Partridge household to discover that their servant had died of smallpox such was the fear of this disease.

Anyone who died other than of old age or illness received a note in the parish record:-

    1747   "Thomas Jenkins a poor man of Wedmore drown'd at Cross Bow."

1753	in July	"a man who died by a fall from his horse coming home from Bristol."
	in August	"he is taken up again and carried home to Clayhanger near Tiverton."
1755	in July	"Amy wife of George Stock died suddenly on ye hill."
	in November	"George died by a fall from a house whilst thatching."

In 1755 the vicar makes a remark in the parish records that seems like disapproval or a reprimand. "Buried this day Mary wife (or should be so) of John Hix". Every child born out of wedlock is noted as a "base" child. The father's name is often included.

Village characters are also to be found noted in the parish register, 1729 "Buried Puss Millard (commonly called, famous for finding hares)" and those who reach a great age, 1806 "buried Mary King age 100 years". At the burial of John Stock the vicar notes that Stock had "served with the King at ye battle of Dettingen". This battle took place during the Austrian war of Succession in June 1733. The allied armies drove the French cavalry in retreat beyond the Rhine. The battle of Dettingen's place in British history is that it was the last occasion in which a king of England (George II) led his troops into battle. F. A. Knight says that records show that John Stock was "wounded in the right thigh at Dettingen and thereby disabled".

Most of these fascinating snippets were added to the records during the time that James Tuthill was vicar of Compton Bishop. Once it became a legal requirement to register births, marriages and deaths the ledgers provided no space for vicars to comment if they felt so inclined.

However even the entries without comment can reveal something about the times in which they were written. Names such as Caple, Day, Fry, Ham, Hardwich, Isgar, Millard, Pym, Sevier, Vowles and Wickham appear as early as the 17th century and many of these families are linked by marriage. For a more complete list of names associated with the parish over several generations see Appendix A.

It is not surprising to see that families often contain a large number of children especially in the Victorian era. Ten children in a family was not uncommon. Thomas and Anne Tilley had eleven children, Charles and Rebecca Caple had twelve, Levi and Hannah Hooper had sixteen.

Like many families in the past, Levi and Hannah had their tragic losses. Two of their children died as infants. This was all too common a story, few families escaped the loss of a child. Today we are shocked to hear of a child's death; so many infectious diseases that could be fatal for children have been prevented or are now curable. How, one wonders, did families cope with the loss of not just one child but several or perhaps the whole family?

In July 1835 Thomas and Eliza Porch of Bourton Farm lost their three children aged five, three and two. Their deaths may have been as a result of an outbreak of some infectious disease in the area as eight infant deaths are recorded in that summer in Compton Bishop church, five including the three Porch children in July. One can imagine, even in a time more used to infant deaths, how stunned such a small community must have been. The Reverend Littlehales must have been only too well aware of the sorrow of his parishioners in 1845 when his own daughter Anna Maria died aged five weeks.

In the corner of Compton Bishop churchyard is the remains of a headstone for Florence Merry who died in 1880 aged five months. The parish records show that William and Mary Merry were to follow a small coffin to the church in 1888 when Elsie died aged eleven months, in 1890 for Wilfred aged six months and again in 1895 when they buried eight month old Ruby. The 1891 census shows that William (he was a carpenter) and Mary were living in Newtown with their son Herbert age ten who appears to be their only surviving child.

The church, as a major landowner, dominated the economic life of much of Somerset. It employed labour, purchased goods, controlled markets and much of agriculture. It also had a major effect on the landscape, its draining projects bringing more land into use for agriculture.

Agriculture has always played an important part in the life of the area. The enclosure of land transformed the appearance of much of the English countryside particularly during the eighteenth century. Large open fields, primarily grazing land, became divided by hedgerows and rhynes. The low lands had always been considered of little value but improved drinage, most noticeable on the levels, made hundreds of acres of land potentially valuable. The enclosure of Cross Moor in 1779 was prompted by its increased worth after improved drainage. Grazing rights were not common to all. The ancient rights to graze on the moors were strictly controlled. These go back to the time when the lord of the manor claimed a measure of work from each tenant. Each small holding was given the right to graze a given number of cattle, or other livestock on common lands.

Once the moor had been divided it was necessary to provide access for each occupier to get to his land without trespassing across a neighbour's land. The commissioners and their surveyors appointed to enclose Cross Moor, drew up a system of droves and these were drawn on to the Plan of Enclosure. Where a drove crossed a river a bridge had to be built. The droves were not public highways and the upkeep was the responsibility of the user of the ground they served.

Enclosure was often prompted by the desire of farmers to take advantage of improvements in agriculture. Better methods of cultivation, the use of fertiliser, new implements and improved livestock from selective breeding were promoted in many areas of the country. In Somerset John Billingsley argued strongly in favour of enclosure. Billingsley (1747 - 1811) who was born at Shepton Mallet published a survey of the agriculture of Somerset in 1795 and devoted much of his life to promoting ideas that would improve agriculture.

The majority of the land in Compton Bishop parish was in the hands of the lord of the manor. William Prowse (see Chapter 2) continued to add to his holding parcels of land in the parish after he acquired the manor. He lived in Axbridge and was probably overseeing the management of his land with the help of a steward. There are records of William Prowse's bailiff collecting dues in 1647.

William's successor, John Prowse, had seven children all of whom were christened in Compton Bishop church. John's surviving son also named John seems to have spent considerable time at Berkley as did his son Thomas. However the connection with Compton Bishop remained strong , the children from these families being baptised and buried in the parish of Compton Bishop or in Axbridge.

By the mid eighteenth century, ownership of the manor was in the hands of the Mordaunt family of Warwickshire. The estate was managed by a steward or bailiff recorded in 1768 as Peter Fry, helped by two moor wardens and a hayward Samuel Gadd, whose job it was to round up stray cattle and put them in the Pound (this was situated in Cross on the north side of the road where the Old Coach Road and Webbington Road meet). The job of bailiff continued to be recorded in the Manorial court book. In 1902 the bailiff was Walter Channon whose father Charles had been bailiff before him. He continued the tradition of dealing with the day to day problems of the tenants; he listened to grievances and gave advice on farming matters. By the end of the nineteenth century independent professional land agents were, for a commission, looking after the detached properties of landowners. It is recorded that A. P. Edwards of Hutton was land agent for the Mordaunt estate up to 1890. His job was the collection of rents and dealing with requests for repairs by tenants.

At the time of the tithe apportionment in 1836, Sir John Mordaunt was the major landowner in the parish of Compton Bishop with eight hundred and fifty acres and was leasing his lands to tenants like the other two major landowners Walter Long with one hundred and thirty one acres and Richard Lowndes with one hundred and eleven acres.

A picture of how the land was used at the beginning of the nineteenth century can also be gained from the details in the tithe apportionment of 1838. The majority of the farmed land was used as pasture. There was a considerable amount of arable particularly at Webbington, around farms and in the centre of Cross between the White Hart and Cleevehead.

Teasels were shown as a crop on which payment of tithes had been made in the past. Teasels had been grown as a field crop in Somerset from early times. The prickly heads, when cut, were dried on long poles propped on a wooden framework called a gallus. It was not an easy crop. Billingsley describes it as "very hazardous" demanding rich soil and good dry weather. Teasels were used to raise the nap on woollen cloth. Long after the local production of wool had declined and production had moved to the steam mills of northern England teasels were still grown in the West Country and transported north. No doubt the teasels that occur on the roadside verges today are the descendants of this forgotten crop.

There is no trace now of the sixty eight separate orchards within the parish listed on the tithe of 1830. Dyke Acland, writing in 1851 states that the favourite apple was the Court of Wick Pippen, a golden pippin on a large handsome, spreading tree. These provided apples for the production of cider drunk in every farm house and given as part of the wage for agricultural workers. Dyke Acland went on to say "the labourer in his year takes off his master's hands about two hogshead of cider; about five percent of his earnings". This practice was popular with the men and with their employer who would rather pay in cider than in cash. Often the practice led to drunkenness and it deprived the family of much needed cash for food and clothes. Dyke Acland went on to say "It refreshes and stimulates him but common cider is not nourishing. The west country labourer will never be what they might as long as this system goes on."

There were eight withy beds. Withies had many uses but most were used to make sheep hurdles, spars for thatching hayricks or baskets. There is a record of a James Parsons, basket maker, living in Cross in 1841. The parish also boasted four nurseries. One situated by the malt house (next to Brewery Farm) and another on the site now occupied by Combe Hay and Monksilver in the Old Coach Road, Cross. Market gardening was to develop during the nineteenth century when the fertile soil at the base of the hill would be used to meet the increasing demand for fresh fruit and vegetables in the expanding towns. The growing of fresh fruit and vegetables was largely unaffected by foreign competition as perishable goods had to be grown close to the market.

By 1851 John Pople, at Newtown, was describing himself as a market gardener; he had eleven acres and was employing one labourer. No doubt most farmers were growing some crop for the fruit and vegetable market by the end of the nineteenth century. The Kelly's Directory of 1861 makes special note that Cross was well known for its production of early peas and potatoes.

By the early years of this century the production of strawberries became popular in the area around Cheddar and Axbridge. Farmers began to grow the crop in rotation with vegetables. The Cheddar valley railway became known as the "strawberry line" when the wagons loaded with baskets of strawberries were attached to the passenger trains. Farmers in Cross took up this new venture but those that thought this was a "get rich quick" idea were soon disillusioned, the crop being so vulnerable to wet weather or droughts.

The Bristol and Exeter Railway opened the Cheddar Valley line in August 1869. (It was to be amalgamated with the GWR in 1876). The coming of the railway provided an opportunity to sell milk, cheese and butter to the fast growing towns. Another profitable crop could be hay since demand for feed for town horses continued to rise during the nineteenth and early twentieth century.

The agricultural depression at the end of the nineteenth century, when increased imports led to a decline in the demand for some crops such as wheat, had little effect on milk producers. Consumer demand for milk was barely satisfied before the urban demand for milk surplus supplies had been turned into butter or cheese by the farmer's wife and sold at local markets. Joseph Harding of Marksbury was the man responsible for producing an accurate recipe that produced a standard cheese of quality that ripened in three months. Somerset was soon widely famed for cheese production which was much prized in London.

Dyke Acland noted in his book The Farming of Somersetshire published in 1851 that "the dairy district south of the Mendip hills and a large proportion of the marshes, are devolved to the making of thick cheese of the finest quality". No particular breed of cow was used on the dairy farms but they were "good sized, long horned and of a mottled red and white colour". He added "Women do all the work. It is true men see the cows milked - but the real hard labour falls to the women; and very industrious they are, but it is a sad sight to see a man standing doing nothing whilst his wife and daughter is turning many times a day a weight above half a hundred weight".

Landowners dominated the life of the countryside for generations. By the nineteenth century it is estimated that three quarters or more of all land was in the hands of wealthy proprietors. Many of these took little or no interest in the day to day life of the communities settled on their estates. They lived off the rents and left farming to their tenants overseen by their steward or bailiff (see page 44).

Towards the end of the nineteenth century, this trend was coming to an end as the depressed state of much of British agriculture led to a fall in land values. Landowners began to sell off much of their land and this was normally offered to their tenants. Many farmers took the opportunity to buy and large parts of landed estates came into the hands of owner occupiers for the first time. There are many deeds for this period contained in the Mordaunt Estate papers boxed in the Warwickshire Records office (unfortunately this large number of documents are mostly unsorted and without an index).

After the manor of Compton Bishop passed to the Mordaunts the lord, in his manor house, was over one hundred miles away in Warwickshire. The Manor Court was still held regularly supervised by the Steward, an influential figure in the community.   With no resident lord of the manor others of social standing and authority within the community of Compton Bishop and Cross would have been the vicar, the doctor and those one or two residents who had the financial resources to enable them to say they were of independent means or titled themselves "gentlemen".

From the tenth or eleventh centuries when parishes were established, the priest became a strong feature in people's lives. Almost everyone went to church, almost all contributed to the support of the church. The clergyman had a high social standing partly because of his spiritual authority and partly because he might be one of the few well educated people in the area.

There is a list of vicars in the porch of Compton Bishop church dating back to 1312. The census returns of the nineteenth century show that William Littlehales (born in Bath) was Vicar of Compton Bishop. He had been living in Compton Bishop from as early as 1833. He probably holds the record for long service, having been vicar of Compton Bishop for fifty seven years.

He lived at the vicarage, built in the late eighteenth or early nineteenth century, with his wife Elizabeth. Their five children were christened in Compton Bishop church between 1838 - 1849. His eldest daughter Amelia was married at the church in 1867 and her five children were also christened there between 1868 - 1879. Like the Hennings at the Rectory (see page 39) family connections with the parish were strong. It is interesting to note that the Hennings and the Littlehales both had connections with the navy. Did William get the living because the Littlehales were known to the Hennings?

William Littlehales died in 1890 aged eighty three. His wife Elizabeth in 1892. They are buried in Compton Bishop churchyard along with one of their daughters Anna Maria, their son Bendall and grand'daughter Maria Bendall Dalton and William's parents.

In such a small rural community it is surprising to find that from early times there was a doctor living and working in the area. In 1799 Henry Harden, surgeon, was taking on a parish apprentice. He probably was living in what is now Newton House.

By 1836 the village doctor was Dr. Wade, living at Cleevehead. Edward Wade was born in 1809 in Henbury, Gloucestershire. He qualified as surgeon of the London College and came to live in Cross in about 1836. He was twenty seven years old and married to his second wife Jane. Jane died in 1839 leaving a two year old son John. Edward remarried the following year to Susannah Wride whose father Francis Wride of Bridgwater was living in Cross at The Cedars. Susannah was twenty three when she and Edward married; they had seven children between 1842 and 1854. Edward became a widower again in 1859 and was by then living at The Cedars.

No doubt needing a mother for at least the youngest of his eight children, Edward married again for the fourth time in 1861. Now aged fifty two he married the thirty one year old Sophia Mills, daughter of William Mills of Cross. Sophia Mills was baptised in Compton Bishop and Dr. Wade must have seen her grow up, perhaps even attended her birth! Edward and Sophia had four children. Sadly despite marrying a woman twenty one years younger than himself Edward was a widower again in 1867 when Sophia died aged thirty seven. He was to remain a widower until his death some twenty three years later.

During his time at The Cedars, Dr. Wade lived a comfortable life with two or three house servants, a stable boy and a groom living in. His working life would have been hard at times. He had to be prepared to tackle every emergency, removing teeth, delivering babies, patching up all types of injuries and carrying out operations in poorly lit cottages. He would have to go out at all hours in his gig or on horseback if the weather made the lanes impassable to wheeled traffic.

The area was fortunate to have had the services of this well qualified man for many years who was, as his tombstone in Compton Bishop churchyard notes; "fifty five years surgeon of this parish". Three of Dr Wade's sons Newton, Charles and Reginald also became physicians.

Dr. Wade was followed by Dr. Arthur Leche who lived at Elmcroft, opposite Townsend Farm. Doctor Leche made up all his own medicines in the surgery, a small room contained shelves of bottles and potions. Older residents remember him as a kindly man who was always willing to come out to the sick at any time. His payment was often a rabbit or a few eggs. He was known to take particular pride in his two seater car. Dr. Leche also remained for many years. His memorial in Axbridge church gives the date of his death as 1949 having been "fifty years physician to Axbridge and District".

The vicar and the doctor would have been known to all in the village. Their professions earning them the respect of everyone in the community and along with a handful of people who were of independent means, they were in effect the "gentry" of the parish. As such they were able to employ servants to run their households and were therefore an important employer of local labour. Employing domestic staff was a sign of social status. During the 19th century the number of people who could afford to employ a servant rose sharply.

Most of those described in the Compton Bishop census are general servants, a maid of all work, especially where only one servant was employed. "A general servant's duties are so multifarious that unless she be quick and active she will not be able to accomplish all" wrote Mrs. Beeton. The census only records "living in " servants and most households would have also employed the daily help of a cook, laundress, gardener and help in the stable from a lad or groom. In 1861 Dr. Wade had three female servants and one male servant living in. Two were general house servants, one a governess and there was also a stable boy. Those that lived in came, in the main, from local villages. At least they would have been able to get to see their families on their half day off unlike those sent to the cities for employment who often lived a lonely life below stairs.

A number of servants came from within the parish and were often very young, several being under sixteen years of age. The youngest recorded being just eleven years old. In 1861 a twelve year old Compton Bishop girl, Hester Lewis, was described as a nursemaid! She was employed by George Tilley and his wife Sarah to help care for their two children aged one and three months. George Tilley ran a boarding School at Crossways House in Cross. He also employed Elizabeth Parsons age seventeen from Compton Bishop as a house servant. How hard they must have worked! Apart from domestic servants most other living in servants were employed as farm labourers or dairymaids.

Those who farmed the largest acreage in any area were almost, but not quite, the lesser gentry. The first half of the nineteenth century had brought prosperity to many farmers who were the major employers of labour. In 1851 Thomas Porch at Bourton Farm with ninety acres was employing eight labourers and had a farm servant living in. George Wickham on a farm which was once on the west side of Compton House, Axbridge with one hundred and thirty acres employed six labourers. They would have also employed additional seasonal labour at haymaking and potato picking including women and children.

Despite the difficult times for farming at the end of the nineteenth century some of the farms and farmers in Compton Bishop were prospering and taking advantage of the opportunity to buy or lease more land. William Toogood, his wife Mary and six children lived in Rackley. The amount of land he farmed rose from one hundred acres in 1851 to one hundred and forty in 1861. Dyke Acland (in 1857) wrote "everything depends upon the industry and economy of the farmer - if he does not get rich, his expenses are small, and he lives in tolerable comfort and plenty". He goes on to mention the importance of the farmer's wife who he describes as "hard working, thrifty and industrious".

The shape of the fields and the layout of the villages of Compton Bishop and Cross have changed very little since the time the tithe map was drawn in 1830 and probably even before then. This is particularly true in Compton Bishop village where only a few houses have been built since 1900. The census shows that almost everyone in Compton Bishop village was employed in agriculture. There does not seem to have been a trade such as blacksmith or even a shop, although there is reference in a directory to Emma Stark being a shop keeper. In many villages a front room was used to sell sweets, haberdashery or other goods and served as a shop.

Some references exist to a tannery in Compton Bishop village. F. A. Knight says it was in the orchard below Manor Farm. The field at the junction of Butts Batch and Vernon's Lane was called Tanyard and in the early nineteenth century there was also a house on the site.

The school was situated in Compton Bishop village on a site now occupied by a house called Longbourne. Plans show a schoolroom thirty feet by fourteen feet six inches plus two rooms nine feet by nine feet and twelve feet by nine feet with a central stairway and hall which served as the school house.

Charity often endowed a village school or money was left in a will for educational purposes. The Cray Charity is one such endowment. William Cray left money from rents of land at Badgworth "for teaching as many poor children of the said parish of Compton Bishop - to read English until perfected therein". Trustees still administer this bequest. The will, dated 1728, says that William Cray lived at Bourton. He ran a school for a while somewhere in the parish. In 1749 the parish register records the burial of Nancy Clark and notes that she had been a teacher at the late Mr. Cray's school. In Cray's handwritten will he writes he is "sick and weak in body but of sound and disposing mind and memory. Thanks be given to Almighty God for same". He then goes into careful detail to dispose of all his worldly goods including his "little red heifer now with calf" to William Middleham of Reckley (sic) and to Thomas Haise of Compton Bishop "my old grey cloth coat and waistcoat to be delivered to him a day or two after my funeral". William Cray died later that year.

National schools were founded in 1811 and used the Monitorial System which enabled one teacher to educate a large number of children of a wide age range. After 1846 most schools had a pupil teacher. These could be as young as thirteen and "should be chosen for character, attainment and special aptitudes". In 1891 Ada Banwell of Compton Bishop was the fourteen year old pupil teacher helping Louisa Bowles, the school mistress. Education was free throughout the country after 1891 and the number of children receiving free education rose to eighty per cent. Earlier education had been almost entirely in the hands of the church. The vicar undoubtedly would have taken a keen interest in the school not only because it was used as a Sunday School but also because education was seen as a means of instilling sober, responsible habits amongst the working classes.

The recurring problem for teachers was poor attendance at school. Even after attendance was made compulsory in 1880 up to the age of ten, certain farming activities led to low numbers as children helped with the farm work or minded younger brothers and sisters whilst mother worked. As late as 1920 the Compton Bishop school log shows the children were given a holiday to pick blackberries. It must have been a long walk for some children to get to school. Bad weather and the lack of shoes or other suitable clothes also led to reduced numbers. Even if they got to school it was often very cold inside the school which was heated by a coal fire. The roof and porch leaked and the "classroom is black in places with damp". The lavatories were described as "unwholesome". Despite these difficulties the school was said to be "promising".

In the early years of the twentieth century, improvements were made, a library was started and a fund to buy a piano. One of the improvements was something of a mixed blessing when in 1922 the playground was concreted. After this there were many reports in the school log of children falling and injuring themselves.

The age of the school children ranged from five to twelve until the leaving age was raised to fourteen. They were taught the three Rs with scripture lessons from the vicar. Practical training was given, the girls learnt to clean and do needlework, the boys learnt gardening. A great deal of coverage is given in the only school log to survive to the work done in the garden. When the school was closed for several weeks after an outbreak of measles, extra time was given to get the garden back to order.

Whatever the standard of education provided by the school in the last century, it would seem that most people could at least sign their name in the marriage register. In 1927 there were over thirty names on the school register. By 1930 Compton Bishop became the junior school, those over eleven years of age going to school in Cheddar. One ex pupil of the 1930's has clear memories of the high ceiling of the schoolroom and the black iron coke fired stove and pine cupboards varnished to an amber glow. The school and schoolhouse were destroyed by a bomb on 2nd September 1940.

The most obvious physical change to the village of Cross is the recent spread of houses and bungalows on the south side of the Old Coach Road and the cutting of a new road in about 1925 from Manor Farm, Cross to Lower Weare. Before this all traffic went through the village which in earlier times was a notable stopping place for the coaching trade. Not surprisingly many people earned their living from this trade. The wheelwright and blacksmith survived the loss of the coach trade brought about by the coming of the railway. They were able to make a living repairing farm machinery and wagons and shoeing the increasing number of horses needed in agriculture and hauling wagons of every kind of trade from the bread van to brewery drays.

The 1841 census shows two blacksmiths in Cross. James Emery was at the Smith's shop on the east side of the White Hart where he lived with his wife and six children. The other blacksmith was William Harse. No trace of any property rented or leased by William Harse has been found and it may be that he worked for Emery living in the other property known to be owned by Emery in the Court (opposite the New Inn). Edward Goldsworthy in his Recollections of Old

Taunton written in 1883 describes the blacksmith in Taunton in his boyhood which would probably be an equally good description of the smithy in Cross. "The blacksmith shop was black, stinking and dirty, with fires blazing, bellows blowing and the hammer and anvil going all day long. At night it gave light to all around."[13] By 1851 Emery was the only blacksmith listed in that census. He was then seventy four years old.

Samuel Burdge also aged seventy four is shown in the same year as a carpenter in Cross. He lived at Moorland Farm with his son Richard and Richard's family. He also occupied the property known now as Fairfields, which is probably where he carried on his trade.

By 1861 Richard Burdge was a blacksmith and carpenter employing four men and a boy. At various times a smith business is shown at Moorland Farm and on the plot between The Cedars and The White Hart. By 1891 Richard Burdge gives his occupation as a farmer and builder. At the turn of the century Richard's sons John and Samuel were running Moorland Farm as a dairy farm.

William Pople was blacksmith by the end of the nineteenth century. Pople had, at one time, also been at the Court. William married Fanny Hellier whose brother Edwin was a carpenter and wheelwright. The wagon repair and blacksmith's business probably linked these families as much as marriage had done.

Edwin Hellier's father David Hellier had been the local carrier until his early death at the age of forty five in 1861. The coming of the railway did not damage local carrier trade. Carriers were an important link with the outside world. They were often the only transport available to those who could not afford coach fares. Servant girls going home, people off to the towns in search of employment used this form of transport. It

57

was a hard way to travel amongst the goods and parcels with perhaps nothing more than a board to sit on. Goldsworthy describes a journey with a carrier from Crewkerne to Taunton. "We started at 12 o' clock at night and reached Taunton about 8 or 9 o' clock next morning. My fellow travellers were a company of strolling players who were to play at Taunton during the Assizes. I slept beside one of the ladies all that dreary night. It was jog, jog, squeak, squeak into ruts and over loose stones."[13]

The nineteenth century saw the establishment of market gardening in Cross. John Pople, from Badgworth, lived at Newtown and in 1841 gave his occupation as an agricultural labourer. By 1851 he had eleven acres of land and was running a market garden. This improved prosperity may well be due to what Dyke Acland described thus in 1851 "It is common practice for farmers to let out portions of land to potato jobbers. Many industrious men have in this way gradually raised themselves to the condition of small farmer". John Pople's son Edward continued the market garden which was thirteen acres in 1881.

Other occupations within the village included shoe makers, Robert Channon who lived with his wife Hester in a cottage part way up Shute Shelve, north of the Arbour Nursing home. There was another family of shoemakers within the parish called Parsons. It may well have been a more common trade in the past using leather from the tannery in Compton Bishop (see page 53).

Carpenters were also to be found. The 1871 census shows two, William Fowles and William Merry as well as a horse-breaker, James Medlam and several gardeners. Also living in the Court from 1851 was a chimney sweep John Say and his wife Alice. Their nine children were all baptised in Compton Bishop church. Widowed John Say married for a second time at the age of sixty two and in 1891 another son Charles was born. John Say died aged eighty in 1907 and is buried with Alice in Compton Bishop.

Just how long there had been a brewery in Cross is uncertain. Though entries in the parish register show that there has been a Collings family in the parish since at least the eighteenth century. The tithe only refers to a malt house but just a few years later James Collings is described in the 1841 census as a maltster and brewer. By 1861 the Collings were farmer, maltster, brewer and employing four men and two boys on ninety nine acres and in 1871 they were employing eight men and two boys on one hundred and forty one acres.

The brewing of cider and beer would have gone on in most houses and farms. It was particularly important at a time when drinking water was often of poor quality. Traditional English ale was made with malt and yeast and it was not until Flemish brewers fled to this country in the fifteenth century that hops were added to make "Bierre". This made a weaker more bitter drink but one which kept longer. The brewing of beer was mainly done by publican/brewers but gradually there emerged families of brewers who supplied local inns and beer houses. The nineteenth century saw a considerable increase in the number of small local brewers though the extent of their market was governed by the range of their delivery wagons. A good brewery's first requirement is good quality water, which was readily available in Cross (see page 8). A ready market for their beer was at hand as Cross had, in the early years of the nineteenth century, three inns with a flourishing trade from travellers.

No picture of the brewery in Cross has so far been found but it was probably much like the brewery in Stogumber which in 1842 was described as a "considerable brewery, the malt liquor from which is held in great estimation; it is said to owe its celebrity in great measure to the peculiar quality of the water". The Times of 1848 said "Stogumber Pale Ale was good for constipation and consumption - and is now drunk by the clergy, gentry and most families throughout England." Collings' beer was said to be the "nut brown ale of old England" and that no cellar was ever without a barrel. The buildings would have almost certainly been of the same distinctive shape as the Stogumber brewery with a tall narrow brewhouse designed to make a maximum use of gravity in the brewing process. The smell of a working brewery is distinctively pungent and yeasty and can last a long time. Many years after brewing ceased in Cross the brewery was used by the Home Guard during World War two when it still smelled strongly of its former use.

The Collings were not without local competition. There were breweries in Banwell (Castles), Cheddar (Budgett) and Axbridge (Fowler). However the consumption of beer and cider, during the nineteenth century, was high especially amongst the working classes. Men, women and children drank beer, often in place of water. The Collings were maltsters as well as brewers. The independent maltster was an important figure. Malted barley was so important that many brewers carried out the malting process near to their brewery. The growing of barley for malting was an important crop in Somerset. A regional report for Somerset County Council in 1934 says some of the best came from near Porlock.

Brewing was labour intensive though much of the work was seasonal. Only once in the Compton Bishop census did anyone give their occupation as a brewer's labourer. James Collings was employing seven men and one boy, but they were also farming 150 acres. Some of these men may have been employed on the farm rather than the brewery, or both.

An essential product for the brewery industry is barrels, and there was a cooper living in Webbington for many years. James Jones was born in Compton Bishop, he gave his occupation as a cooper at the baptism of his first child in 1839. James Jones and his wife Temperance (nee Wickham) had a further seven children baptised in Compton Bishop church. James Jones was still giving his occupation as a cooper in 1891. Was he still making barrels at the age of seventy six? An 1844 directory lists three coopers. One in Cheddar and two in Axbridge. One of these was George Norwell who lived within Compton Bishop parish in West Street, Axbridge.

It is said the firm of J. J. Collings (James and John and later with William Edward) was taken over by Holts of Burnham (1770 - 1957). Holts succumbed to Starkey, Knight and Ford (1895 - 1962) who in turn were taken over by Whitbreads. People still remember the Starkey, Knight and Ford emblem, a large black horse painted on the wall of the New Inn, and they may well have taken over the houses selling Collings beer at the same time as the brewery. All that remained of the brewery was incorporated into a riding stable. Today the house called Brewery Farm is all that can be seen of the old brewery. It is one of the most attractive old buildings in Cross.

Cross also boasted a saw yard. Situated opposite Manor Farm, Cross it was occupied by Charles Channon in the 1860s and wood from Kingswood or Rosewood was prepared here for the Mordaunt estate for local farmers. The site of the saw yard, like that of the post office, disappeared when the new road (the A38) was cut.

Before 1805 all mail went to a receiving house in Axbridge. From 1806 letters were sorted at Axbridge and delivered by a "walk postman" covering the route from Axbridge via Cross, Loxton, Bleadon, Uphill and Weston-super-Mare and back. A receiving house was established in Cross in 1827 to which general letters could be rated.[14] The site of the post office was close to Manor Farm,Cross. The 1841 census shows the post mistress was Mary Gibbons. The postman, who lived in Cross, was Silas Godby. Silas would have been a familiar figure to everyone. He and his wife Frances had six of their seven children whilst living in Cross, the youngest Joseph arriving in the year Silas was 40.

The Somerset Constabulary was formed in 1856. In the later nineteenth century a policeman lived in Cross near to the post office, the exact location is uncertain. By 1881 the police house was Bridle Cottage on the east side of the White Hart.

There were several quarries within the parish of Compton Bishop. Reeve Hay, North Batch, Dunnett and Outing Batch. The one that has left the most visible impact is the quarry in Cross. There are many recordings of men whose occupation was concerned with the quarry or its products; Quarryman, Limeburner, Stonecutter and Stonebreaker. The quarry was an important source of employment. From earliest times these quarries would have provided stone for buildings or enclosures but undoubtedly the main use for the stone quarried within the parish was for roadstone and lime. The Surveyor of Highways, William Mills, records in 1836/37 that he was responsible for seven miles of highway. He spent sixty four pounds sixteen shillings and ninepence and employed three to five men to scrape the roads, repair the sides and spread stones for two shillings (ten new pence) a day. One third of his expenditure was on wages, the rest went on materials, tools and contracting a horse and cart.

The amount of work done in quarries can be gauged by the fact that William Mills carefully noted that George Paine and Richard Marshall quarried ninety tons of stone in the five weeks of April,1863 at sixpence a ton. A bill for four pounds eight shillings and tenpence halfpenny to a tradesman "for blasting" indicates that stone was blasted from the rock face. At Cross Quarry stones were loaded into small wagons called putts which went up and down the steep slope to the road beside Cleevehead. At the road men sat on piles of sacks breaking stones into small pieces with a hammer before it was taken away by horse and cart. The amount of stone prepared varied according to the weather conditions but averaged about seven tons a week. For this the men earned eight pence a ton. More stone was quarried than could be used on parish roads, the surplus no doubt sold by the Mordaunt Estate. The quarry does not seem to have come into private hands until about 1897 when Albert Pople states he is a farmer with forty acres and quarry owner employing six men and two boys.

F. A. Knight notes that the quarries in the area were used extensively to obtain lime for burning. The quarry in Cross contained a lime kiln, the remains of which can still be seen to the west of the gated entrance to the quarry. A description of a lime kiln by Billingsley would probably have equally served for those in Cross "their form is of a French bottle, the height seventeen feet, the length of the neck, in which the calcination is wholly affected, seven feet; its diameter four feet and the diameter of the belly in the largest part twelve feet". Lime had become popular in the eighteenth century as an "improver" of soil. Billingsley attributed improvements of cultivation in great measure to the application of lime. "Soon after harvest, indeed at any part of the winter, liming is begun. Four horses and two men with two carts holding thirty two bushels of lime each will cover one acre in half a day".

Few shops existed in villages before the mid nineteenth century. The earliest indication of a shop in a form which would be familiar to us today in the parish of Compton Bishop is in the Kelly's Directory of 1840. This does not mean that trade in goods and perishables was not going on within the villages. A room in a cottage, a barn or an outbuilding might be used to trade in produce, paraffin or haberdashery. In 1844 Thomas Davey describes himself as a grocer and was living at or near the old post office (now demolished see page 61). Perhaps then as now the post office was also a general stores. Before the advent of the village shop, supplies were often obtained from travelling packmen, tinkers for pots and pans or pies and gingerbread from hawkers. The carrier brought in goods from the towns. Coal was landed at Rackley. In 1766 the overseer of the poor was paying nine shillings (forty five pence) for "hauling ten bushels of coal from Rackley to the Poor House". It was not far to the market held in Axbridge on Tuesday and Saturday and there was also a wide range of shops in Axbridge. The 1859 directory lists a chemist, draper, ironmonger, baker, butcher, a hairdresser, a tailor and watch and clock maker.

Those on low income and most people within the parish were on low incomes, had little need of many shops. Their diet consisted mainly of bread and potatoes, meat of any kind was a rare luxury in the 19th century, thirty percent of labourers' families never ate meat. Most food was produced at home from vegetables and potatoes from the garden or from the vegetable plot. The most likely weekly purchase would be bread, sugar and tea. Tea and sugar, once former luxuries, were the main reason for the arrival of the village store and Emma Stark and George Escott Vowles and Charles Vowles all, at some time, describe themselves as shopkeepers by the end of the nineteenth century. The village shop in Cross was run for many years by Mrs. Keen. Born in Compton Bishop, Louisa Keen was one of the eleven children of Evan and Elizabeth Baden. At her marriage in 1853 to George Keen Louisa gave her occupation as a dressmaker. They had seven children the last of whom James died age two years in 1867, the same year that Louisa, now age forty one, became a widow. By the time of the 1871 census Louisa Keen was running a general grocery store in Cross. Mrs. Keen would have undoubtedly been an able woman, "grocers had to understand how to choose, blend, grind, weigh and package most of their stock."[15] Shopkeepers were expected to extend credit to all and it required tact and a firm hand to get payments from customers.

Louisa Keen's son John became a master baker, another son Robert was a butter dealer who went on to be a carrier with a route into Weston-super-Mare every Tuesday and Friday. He married Elizabeth, daughter of John Bowden, the gardener at Compton Bishop Vicarage.

Up to quite recent times the head of many households within the parish was an agricultural worker. In the 1851 census there are seventy six men who give their occupation as an agricultural worker. The oldest being James Vowles aged seventy two. Until the years just before the first world war almost all farm tasks were performed by hand. Agriculture was one of the largest employers of labour and although this was to decline during the end of the nineteenth century as people left to seek employment in the towns, parishes such as Compton Bishop were still firmly wedded to agriculture.

In 1891 William Stark was just such an agricultural worker living in one of the cottages on the south side of the village school (the cottage is now called Honeysuckle Cottage). William and his wife Emma were both born in Compton Bishop. William, born about 1849, was one of the four children of John and Hester Stark. William's wage as an agricultural worker would have been about nine shillings (forty five or fifty pence) per week. In addition he almost certainly got extras such as potatoes, vegetables or milk. He very probably also received a cider allowance as part of his earnings. From his wages William Stark's main expenditure would have been the seven pounds and three shillings (Seven Pounds and Fifteen Pence) a year rent for his cottage (information from the Mordaunt papers). This left the family, they had eight children, with less than twenty pounds a year for food, fuel, clothes and other expenses. Any additional income was obviously of great value and it is quite likely that William's wife Emma was able to earn a few pence washing, sewing or on a seasonal farm task.

Everyone, who was able, helped in the fields at hay-making or harvest. Children were expected to help as soon as they were old enough to look after themselves. "They were sent to scare birds, stop cattle straying. Glean, gather potatoes, pick mushrooms or blackberries, pick up cider apples, bring home firewood."[16] As soon as they were old enough the children went into full time work. If this was away from home it eased the strain on often overcrowded cottages. By 1891 three of the Stark children had left home, Elizabeth age fifteen and John age seventeen appear to have left the parish whilst Henry age eighteen was living at Compton House,Cross as a farm servant to Charles Tilley. It is impossible to say for certain what conditions were like in William Stark's cottage. Many were living in very poor accommodation "There is a strong and just feeling among tenants that landlords ought to do more to provide the labourers with decent cottages" (Dyke Acland). By the standards of the time the Stark's cottage may have been quite good as the Mordaunts seemed to have had a caring attitude towards their cottagers. Land was set aside in Compton Bishop for allotments to encourage tenants to be more self sufficient. The rules set out by Sir Charles Mordaunt forbade gardening on a Sunday and any tenant "who habitually neglected attending church, no drunkard, swearer, immoral or dishonest person will not be allowed to retain his garden". The site of the allotments is now occupied by the council houses.

Particularly during Victorian times romantic myths about the countryside grew up and persisted for many generations. The picture of a thatched cottage with a garden full of flowers occupied by a cheerful rosy cheeked family was the generally held impression of the life of the working classes in the English countryside. In truth if they had employment, accommodation and were fit and healthy, they got by. Any unfortunate circumstances would soon find a person or family in real difficulty.

From the fifteenth century the parish gradually began to take over from the manorial court and became in effect a unit of local government. Known as the Vestry, it took its name from the church room in which the meetings usually took place. The Vestry was headed by the Vicar and Churchwarden and wielded considerable power. The officers were charged with law and order, for which they appointed the constable. Care of roads in the parish, other than the turnpike, was the concern of the Surveyor of the Highways and dealing with social problems fell to the Overseer of the Poor. But nineteenth century changes and legislation were to have a major impact. The 1834 Poor Law Act, the civil registration of births, marriages and deaths in 1837 and the setting up of Boards of Health all combined to reduce the responsibility of the parish.

In Compton Bishop much time seems to have been spent finding sufficient persons to serve as officers of the vestry. From the rate, which in 1811 was two shillings and threepence (eleven pence) the vestry spent the recorded sum of one hundred and nine pounds four shillings and two pence (one hundred and nine pounds and twenty one pence) on relieving the poor and distressed, the upkeep of the poor house and the roads in the parish. The records of the meetings show

Sir John Mordaunt attended the Vestry meetings in 1771 and 1781.

The overseer of the poor was called upon to provide for a wide variety of needs such as:-

    1766 - for clothing George Marshals daughter before she went to service £1..15s..0d (£1.75).

    1767 - John Elvers paid eight shillings and sixpence (42.5p) for making clothes for the Hardwidge boys. A later entry shows the cost of a pair of breeches was one shilling and eightpence (8p).

    1785 - The cost of a child's coffin was five shillings (25p). John Swearse was the coffin maker.

Money for medical expenses occur in several forms:-

    1782 - a poor man "with an apsiss (sic) was given sixpence" (2.5p).

    1785 - John Methuen had to be taken to Bath Hospital at a cost of twelve shillings and sixpence (62.5p). His wife, children and rent all fell upon the parish. "Ye apothecary's bill" for John Methuen was £16..11s..10d. A huge outlay for the parish to find.

    1780 Mary Allin was given one pint of brandy and one quart of wine in childbed which cost the parish four shillings and fourpence. A further ten shillings and sixpence was expended for attending at her time of labour.

Payments were often made for alcohol (wine or brandy) for the sick. This seems to have been an ominous sign as it is often followed by an entry that the parish was now to provide a funeral. Clearly alcohol was provided when the end was thought to be in sight. Doubtless some received this comfort and went on to survive. There were costs for official duties such as five shillings (25pence) for a man and horse to attend the coroner at Bridgwater after a man hanged himself in 1793. In 1785 it was necessary to send a person to the prosecution of William Styles "who murdered ye lad near Shoot Shelve (sic) and was hanged for same".

From the time of Elizabeth I attempts were made to provide poor relief. An Act of Parliament required every parish to appoint an overseer of the poor. His job was to find work for those unemployed and supply funds for sudden emergencies. The money came from a rate levied on all property owners.

A poor house was constructed in Compton Bishop to which families in distress could be sent. This house was in the corner of the churchyard near the site of the present noticeboard. It was built of stone with a roof thatched with helms (straw thatch). The overseer's book refers to the maintenance of the building, especially the roof, and the purchase of lime for the walls. There are also many references to families and their goods being "hauled to the poor house". For some families staying in the poor house was a regular occurrence. In the early 1800's the Bidwell family were often in receipt of help to pay for lodgings, for bread and potatoes and two shillings for children's clothes and finally in 1814 the whole family found themselves in the poor house. It was pulled down in 1840 and the materials sold to the highest bidder.

Another attempt to deal with poverty and at the same time help to relieve the parish of some of the financial burden, was binding poor children as apprentices. There was no minimum age limit for apprentices until 1816. Boys were bound until age twenty four, girls until age twenty one or marriage. Any person within the parish might be required to take an apprentice and they could be fined five pounds for refusing. Probably few declined as it was a source of cheap labour. Two of the Bidwell children, Hannah and Elizabeth, were appointed to local farmers in 1814 at the time when the family were moved to the poor house. The Callow children, Peter, Rachael, Mary and William were all placed as apprentices in 1834. Later the same year the overseer was looking "to procure a place as apprentices on some merchant ship" for William Callow and his brother Henry aged about twelve and nine.

The number of people receiving relief throughout the country grew and grew as did complaints from those within the community on whom a rate was levied to pay for poor relief. There were those who felt the poor were just workshy and that parish relief was pampering the feckless. In 1834 the Poor Law Act proposed the merging of parishes into Unions run by a committee of elected ratepayers to be called the Guardians of the Poor. At its heart the Union was to contain the workhouse.

Austerity was the keynote for the workhouse. They had a prison like appearance with high walls and small high windows which cut the inmates off from the outside world. Inside the poor slept on cheap wooden beds; pillows were not provided. The only other furniture was rough tables and benches at which meals were taken. There were no comfortable chairs, even for the elderly and no books or games. There were many rules and regulations. Punishment for breaking rules was often harsh and in some workhouses it was brutal. Separation of the sexes was total so that families admitted to the workhouse were split up. Infants were, however, permitted to remain with their mothers. On admission all inmates were issued with coarse clothing which was in effect the 'paupers uniform'. Inmates were given tasks to perform. Corn grinding, bone grinding, stone breaking and picking oakum and of course all the necessary work required to run the workhouse. There was a legal requirement to provide medical attention. The workhouse hospital became, in effect, the poor people's infirmary. The bleak institutions that sprang up all over the country with their harsh regimes were designed to deter people from seeking relief.

The Axbridge Union was formed on 28th January 1838. Included in the Union was the parish of Compton Bishop and many others over a wide area from Blagdon to Highbridge, Weston-super-Mare to Cheddar. The workhouse was built in Axbridge and remained until unions were abolished in 1929. It can still be seen, converted now into flats. The person upon whom, more than anyone else, the day to day life of the workhouse inmates depended was the workhouse master. In 1840 the Master of the Axbridge Workhouse had the memorable name of Onisephorus Millard. As was a common practice his wife Mary Ann was the workhouse matron. They were responsible for a frequently changing variety of inmates (two hundred and fourteen at the 1841 census) who might include amongst their number, whole families, lunatics, tramps, the sick, the elderly, unmarried mothers and new born infants. By the standard of the time Axbridge Workhouse appears to have had a reasonable regime. The punishment book survives from 1864 - 1897. "Crimes" include refusing to work, fighting, absconding, insulting the Master and refusing to wash. One man is reported to have said "he would not take off his shirt for any man" when told to wash himself. In contrast to reports beginning to circulate in some parts of the country about workhouse punishments Axbridge seems quite mild. Mostly offenders were locked up for six or twelve hours or were put on bread and water. Birching and caning were carried out on several occasions by the workhouse schoolmaster for stealing, absconding or on one occasion for "brutally killing a cat".

The workhouse schoolmaster and schoolmistress in 1861 were James and Elizabeth Salisbury; their combined salary was £17..12s..6d (£17.62) per year. James came from Axbridge and Elizabeth (nee Gully) from Shipham. They married in Compton Bishop in 1844 and had four children. Herbert, Hubert, Samuel and Betha all baptised in Compton Bishop Church. By 1871 James and Elizabeth had become Workhouse Master and Matron.

In 1861 there were one hundred and seventy persons in the workhouse and one hundred of these were under fifteen years of age. It is uncertain what age range received some form of schooling in the workhouse but clearly there was plenty of work for the teachers. Those old enough and fit enough were expected to work. For the women it was picking oakum (unravelling ropes, often tar covered). The men broke stones under the archway that led to the tramps ward. The Guardians were reported to be unhappy about the work being done as they considered it to be no real task.

There were between twenty five and thirty four births per year in Axbridge Workhouse between 1838 - 1847 which would include two or three illegitimate children. Single mothers fared worse than most under the Poor Law. The support of a child born out of wedlock fell to the mother as she was easy to identify; the father got off scot free. It was thought that focusing on the women in this way would act as a deterrent to becoming pregnant. If she had no family to support her she must enter the workhouse or starve. The bare facts noted in the Axbridge Workhouse log conjure up the tragedy of these women and their babies. Like the details of Jane Franklyn who entered Axbridge Workhouse in November 1874. Her child Emily was born in February 1875 and Jane died in March. One wonders what became of Emily.

Axbridge Workhouse had a cook and a baker. Contracts were issued for the purchase of meat, flour, rice, salt, butter, cheese, peas and oatmeal. Oatmeal was used to make the standard workhouse breakfast, a thin porridge known as gruel.

There was clearly some respite from the tedium of day to day life in Axbridge Workhouse. A band was formed and went out to play at local events. It was to be seen as a reward for good behaviour to be allowed to play in the band or to be one of the twelve boys allowed to drill with the local Rifle Corps. At Christmas roast beef and plum pudding was provided. Extra funds were found so that the inmates were able to celebrate the marriage of the Prince of Wales in 1862.

> "It was Christmas Day in the workhouse
> And the old bare walls are bright
> With garlands of green and holly.
> And the place is a pleasant sight;
> For clean washed hands and faces,
> In a long and hungry line
> The paupers sit at the tables
> For this the hour they dine."
>
> George R. Sims

Over the years there grew up a hatred and fear of the workhouse especially amongst the elderly. A stay in the workhouse was at best of short duration for most able bodied people. For the old, privations of the workhouse were particularly stressful. There was no recognition of their special needs until the end of the nineteenth or early twentieth century. Most of all the elderly feared dying in the workhouse. Parish relief was often a way of life for the elderly and many needed help at some time or the other. Usually it was impossible to save even a few pennies during a lifetime of work. Active men and women were often able to support themselves wholly or in part by continuing to work in old age.

The census details of 1841 show William Caple age seventy three and Joseph Tripp age seventy five both still working as agricultural labourers, Martha Pyther age seventy nine was keeping poverty at bay by working as a charwoman. Older still, Edward Caple eighty seven (sturdy stuff these Caples!) and Samuel Jones aged an amazing ninety four were labourers in 1861.

It was an often expressed wish that "The good Lord would take them before they became a burden to anyone". Parishes had always tried to provide a dignified funeral for young and old if the family were unable to do so.

In the Overseer of the Poor's accounts there are many references to money paid out for various items required at burial:-

    1767 a coffin for widow of Richards ten shillings.
    1782 One gallon of ale at burying of Martha Richards.
    1784 Payment to Sexton three shillings and sixpence for grave digging.
    1811 Paid eight poor men to carry Peter Medlam to his grave from Axbridge to Compton Bishop three shillings.
           Tolling of bell one shilling and sixpence.
           Funeral cost one pound and fifteen shillings.
    1816 One shilling and sixpence given to a man for his wife's shroud.

To make a little extra money families frequently took in a lodger. James Hardwitch (sixty seven) and his wife Sophia (seventy) had three lodgers. This was sometimes a kindly gesture to keep elderly people from having to enter the workhouse. In 1841 James Vowles aged sixty five and his wife Grace had two paupers Ann Masters seventy seven and Grace

Stock seventy nine living with them. It is interesting to note that the census records paupers within the community.

Sharing a cottage between two families was not uncommon. Once the children had grown up and had children of their own grandchildren frequently came to live easing the burden in a crowded home. In 1881 John Bowden age seventy four (still working ten years later as the vicarage gardener) shared his home with his daughter, granddaughter and a seventy year old lodger. Elderly grandparents, in turn often went to live with the family once they were too old to live alone or unable to work to pay their rent. Henry Amesbury and his wife Lucy were sharing their home with an elderly mother and Henry's forty one year old brother William described as a "Pauper idiot".

The Outdoor Relief Order of 1852 laid down that assistance could be given to the able bodied outside the workhouse. At least half of any assistance must be food, fuel or other necessary articles. These items were purchased by the Guardian of the Poor on contract and always at the lowest tender.

One attempt to help people help themselves was the establishment in 1836 of the Axbridge and West Mendip Friendly Society. Its aim was to encourage "among the working classes habits of Industry, Forethought and Self Support by affording means of assuring a provision for Infancy, Sickness and Old Age, and Upon Death".

There were four classes of payment and relief. At age twenty one - ten pence per month would insure a weekly allowance of four shillings (20p) in times of sickness. There were payments in old age of two shillings (10p) per week and a death grant of four pounds. Endowment for children of sixpence (2.5p) per month from age one year would produce six pounds at age fourteen or money returned if the child died.

Medical and surgical attendance was covered by an additional payment of three shillings (15p) per year. This was split into two payments of one shilling and sixpence (7.5p) payable in March and September. The patrons of the Society were the Marquis of Bath, the Bishop of Bath and Wells and Sir John Mordaunt.

Many people sought a new life and better opportunities in the expanding towns and cities as the agricultural depression deepened. Those with a taste for adventure looked to the new world for a new and better life. America and Canada had been attracting emigrants for many generations. Australia however carried the stigma of a convict colony for many years. Landowners in Australia began to use agents in the west country to seek out people with the skills they needed. The British Government set up the Wakefield System of assisted emigration to encourage those who were "sober, industrious and of good moral character" to settle in Australia.

Samuel and John Hardwidge of Compton Bishop emigrated to Australia in 1856. Samuel was thirty years old, he and his wife Eliza had two children Hester age four and Emily age two. John was his younger brother aged twenty six. He and his wife Mary Ann had one child four year old Rebecca.

They probably travelled to Plymouth where they would have awaited the departure of their ship at the emigrants home. The conditions on ships travelling to Australia controlled by the British Government were generally better than those that crossed the Atlantic. Nevertheless the family had little space or privacy on a journey that would take between five to seven months.

The Hardwidge families arrived at Port Phillip on board the ship Sabrina on 14th April 1857 to begin their new life in Victoria a state more than fifty five times larger than the county of their birth. They were assigned to Mr. Duncan, a farmer at Bulleen where they worked for rations and a wage larger than they had received at home. Later Samuel Hardwidge lived with his wife and three children in Bulleen Road, Doncaster and then went to Croydon where three more children were born. This area had been largely ignored by settlers until around the 1870's. Fortunately there were many trees which were soon put to use for houses and later railway construction.

Samuel took up a grant of one hundred and one acres of land in 1881 which was worked mainly as orchards. The plot of land contained an elevated section and it was on this that the family home was built. The Hardwidge acreage developed as a valuable property as the apex of the triangle adjoined the railway property. Samuel died in 1912 leaving a will directing that his five living children receive a life interest in his estate.[17] It was therefore many years before the plot was divided up and streets bearing names of the family and the county they came from - Hardwige Street, (The spelling changed in Australia) Samuel Street, Emily Crescent and Somerset Crescent appeared on the land. Samuel's brother John and his wife Mary Ann had seven more children in Australia. The Hardwidge family in Australia now totalled eighteen. This family tree was to bear many branches. In 1957, one hundred years after Samuel and John arrived in Australia, four hundred and fifty of the known seven hundred and fifty descendants of the Hardwidge family turned up for a reunion party in Cheong Park in Croydon, Victoria. Such was the scale of the event it received prominent coverage in the local paper.

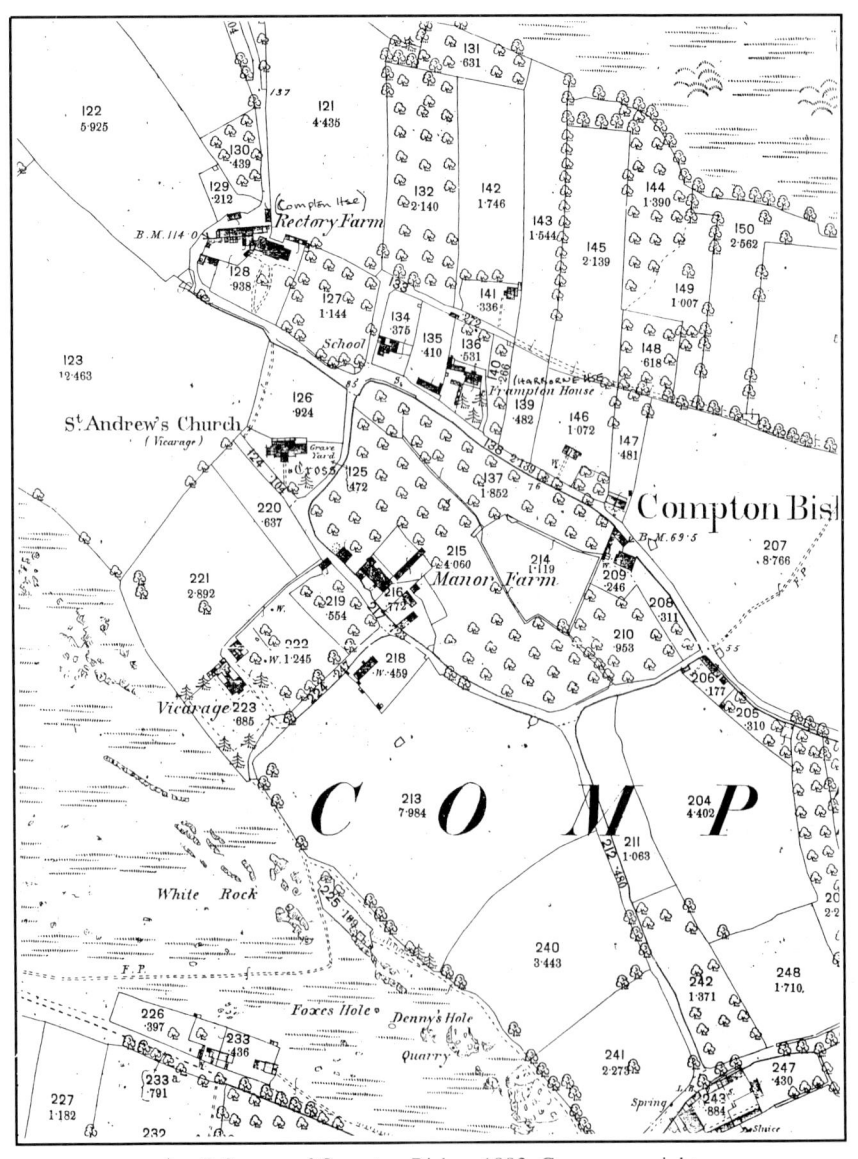

▲ O.S. map of Compton Bishop 1883. Crown copyright.

▲ 25. The Cedars, Dr. Wade's home for many years.

26. Brewery Farm, all that remains of the brewery at Cross. ▼

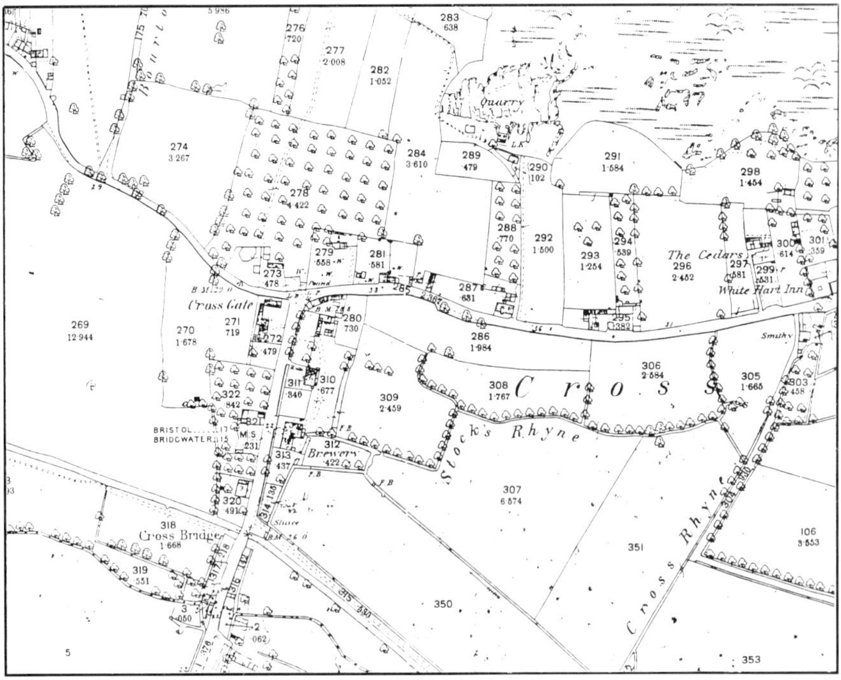

▲ O.S. map showing part of Cross 1883. Crown copyright.

27. Cross, the village shop can be seen on the right. (Date unknown). ▼

▲ 28. St. Andrews Church, Compton Bishop.

29. The Bells of St. Andrews Church prior to being re-hung in 1938. ▼

▲ 30. Honeysuckle Cottage, Compton Bishop.

31. The Quarry, Cross. ▼

▲ 32. Dr. Arthur Leche.

▲ 33 & 34. Two photographs of the Tilley family outside Compton House, Axbridge. (Dates unknown).

▲ 35. Cross, Manor Farm and Cross Lane, lined with elm trees. (Date unknown).

36. Board of Guardians, Axbridge Union Workhouse 1930. ▼

When I began looking into the history of the parish I was uncertain how far back I would be able to go. I also decided to limit research into more recent times to no later than the beginning of this century. However a number of items from the 20th century emerged that I thought should not be left out. This resulted in the following final chapter

WITHIN LIVING MEMORY

Topiary

The celebrated topiary in the front garden of The Yews, Cross attracts many visitors. The house, once known as Avalon has been in the Smith family since 1842 and it was the present owner's great grandfather who, before 1895, planted four of the six trees that form the huge spires that can be seen today.

Webbington House

Designed by the architect E. J. May, Webbington House was built of stone from Loxton Quarry in 1908 for Mr. Herman Tiarks. Mr. Tiarks was Patron of the living of Loxton and Joint Master (with his brother Frank) of the Weston Harriers. He married Jessie Follet of Winscombe Court in 1901. It was Mrs.Tiarks who was largely responsible for creating ornamental gardens where only fields had previously existed.

The house was approached by a long driveway flanked by roses. The four acre garden had sloping lawns and terraces. Rose walks led to arbours and shrubberies of yew, box and fuchsia behind which were the lawns for games and the tennis courts. There was a fine chestnut tree and several walnut trees.

Webbington House is now a hotel.

World War I

The new century was less than two decades old when World War I began in 1914. All over the country men signed up to fight a war that they thought would be over by Christmas. From the parish of Compton Bishop eighty two men, recorded on the roll of honour of St. Andrews Church, went off to fight during the next four years. Seven of these men did not return.

One of those who died was Dr. Leche's son. Second Lieutenant Victor Leche died on 1st July 1916 at the battle of Beaumont Hamel. This was the first battle on the first day of the battle of Somme. The battle had begun at 7.30 a.m. on a fine warm morning, the fighting on that first day gained no ground for the British forces who sustained heavy losses. Only two officers remained on duty at the end of the day. The rest, some twenty six officers, including Victor Leche, were dead or wounded along with four hundred and thirty eight other ranks. There is no record on how twenty year old Victor Leche died. He was listed as missing presumed dead. His memorial in Compton Bishop church says he died "leading his men in the great assault on German lines".

The loss of men to the armed services must have led to a shortage of manpower on the farms in Compton Bishop and Cross that were at full stretch for the war effort. Fields were ploughed for extra crops and hay was grown to feed the huge number of horses that were sent to the battlefields, many of these horses having been requisitioned from the farms.

Bourton Farm was for a time an army remount centre. Six hundred mules were brought to the farm. The soldiers who were to look after the mules were barracked in the hay barns. The summer was very wet and the mules churned up the land so much that it looked as if it had been ploughed. Before the mules arrived many of the fine elm trees on Bourton Farm were painted with tar to prevent the mules chewing and thereby causing the probable death of the tree.

When peace eventually came to a war weary Britain in November 1918 local Armistice Day celebrations were held in Cross brewery!

It was not long before the men who returned from the war to "a land fit for heroes" were to find the country gripped by strikes, unemployment and hunger marches. These difficult years must have had an effect on Compton Bishop and Cross but the only record is a note made by the headmistress of Compton Bishop School in the school log in 1921 "There is no coal for the school fire due to the coal strike. There are severe snow storms and it is very cold so the children were sent home".

The Cross Diversion

The road through Cross ceased to be a turnpike road when the Bristol Trust was wound up in 1867. The Local Government Act of 1888 placed responsibility for main roads on the new county councils. In the mid 1920's Somerset County Council decided to make a new road from the base of Shute Shelve Hill across part of Cross Moor to Lower Weare by-passing the village of Cross.

Constructing roads across the Somerset levels has always been difficult due to the soft wet conditions on the moors.

Older residents recall that part of the construction of the road called for cart loads of hazel twigs to be delivered. These were made into bundles known as fascines and were used to form the base on which the road could be constructed. The bridges were piled but even today the road is inclined to sink and has to be regraded from time to time.

Cross was no longer on the main road and most travellers ceased passing through the village as they had done for centuries. Nobody in the 1920's or 30's could possibly have foreseen the volume of traffic that would be using the main road (now the A38) some sixty years later, which without the Cross diversion would have had to travel through the village.

World War II

Twenty one years after the end of World War I Britain was at war again. The threat of invasion was real and many security measures were in place. Huge obstacles were placed beside the bridge in the Old Coach Road. In the event of invasion these were to be put on the bridge to block off the road. No-one seemed sure how these were to be lifted! A local defence force known at first as Local Defence Volunteers (LDV) and later the Home Guard was set up in 1940. The area headquarters was at Weston-super-Mare until 1943 when an Axbridge battalion was formed out of part of the Weston-super-Mare battalion. The disused brewery in Cross served as a Home Guard post.

Once again the countryside was called upon to produce extra food and additional land was put to the plough. The Women's Land Army was formed to replace male farm workers who were away in the armed forces. Courses were organised at Badgworth to teach the skills of thatching. Later

Italian prisoners of war were a familiar sight on farms in the area. Many people recall the Italian prisoner who worked at Moorland Farm. Known as Vinci he lived in the farmhouse and took his meals in the kitchen with the family. Although a prisoner of war he was "trusted" and got on with his work unsupervised. After the war Vinci returned to Italy and married. He and his wife later returned to England and settled in Weston-super-Mare.

The first evacuees arrived in 1940 and were billeted with families within Compton Bishop and Cross. Their arrival "required much patience to mix town and country bred amicably together."[18] The increased number of children put pressure on the school, in temporary accommodation since being bombed, which was forced to work a shift system. Some went to school in the morning others in the afternoon. The evacuees must have found country life vastly different but many have returned to visit the area and leave their names in Compton Bishop church visitors book. John Kaley was only nine years old when he was evacuated to Compton Bishop vicarage. He recalls how he loved to walk the hills which he thought were the top of the world. "Imagine all this for a kid from Dagenham." His parents however were not so sure Compton Bishop was safe for him. After coming to stay they described the noise of aircraft overhead at night as worse than Dagenham! Syd Mercer was evacuated to the parish in 1943 when he was twelve years old. He was billeted at number one the council houses. He recalled being shocked to find they had no electricity. However he loved the freedom to roam the countryside, playing with the village children in the river and climbing the many cider apple trees. He had never seen an orchard before coming to the village.

About twenty five children, mostly from London, were billeted at Webbington House the home of Henry Tiarks. They occupied the top floor of the house and were cared for by Mrs. Slim the matron who came from Lower Weare. Mrs. Slim said when interviewed in 1992 that she looked back on that time as happy and rewarding though caring for twenty five children aged between five and fifteen years of age was hard work; especially the washing and managing all their ration books!

Those who have returned to the place where they were evacuated have mostly happy childhood memories of experiencing the new freedom of the countryside but the war was never far away. Ralph Millage who was seven years old when he began a four year stay in the area said that one of his most vivid memories was looking up through the big elm tree that once stood at the corner of Church Road and seeing in the distance "hundreds of aircraft flying in formation".

The area was to experience the effects of bombs and a crashed aircraft. A Spitfire crashed near Axbridge station on 27th April 1942 killing the pilot.The first local bomb crater at Weare was the source of much curiosity "one Sunday morning we all trailed across the fields to see what had happened, and even contributed to the Red Cross collecting boxes of the nurses for the privilege of seeing it."[18]

In September 1940 a bomb made a direct hit on Compton Bishop School and School House and totally demolished them causing a huge crater. Miss Gunton, the matron of the Home, (see Page 86) interviewed in 1992, recalling the night the school was hit said she was awoken by a terrific noise and blinding flash of light. Having checked everyone in her charge was safe she set about organising cocoa for everyone. There was an unexpected loud knocking at the door which when opened revealed Mrs. Howell, the school mistress, with her daughter and her mother. They were all covered in dust. It was only then that Miss Gunton realised that the school had been hit. Mrs. Howell and family had been sleeping in the school house at the time of the explosion and had miraculously escaped injury. The only casualty was the family dog. (The same explosion also damaged the glass in the church windows).

A temporary school was set up in Mr. Amos's garage (at a house now known as Glastonbury Thorn) and it was not until June the following year that new accommodation was found for the children at Cross Memorial Hall. The fifty one children on the register must have found it very cramped in the hall which also had to double as a function centre for the many fund raising efforts of the war years.

The villages of Compton Bishop and Cross were busy throughout World War II collecting household waste such as paper, bones, tins, rags and rubber for recycling for the war effort. A Women's Institute "Jam Centre" operated in the shed at the Pound (see page 45) Using locally grown fruit, especially blackberries from the hedgerows, thousands of pounds of jam were dispatched to the cities.

Large amounts of money were raised for Weapons Weeks in July 1941 when Axbridge Rural Districts aimed to raise £35,000 the cost of seven fighters "in order to help in the ultimate hanging of Hitler and his fiendish friends". In 1942 efforts to raise even more money were again underway. This time it was for Warship Week when the eleven parishes that made up Axbridge Rural District had a target of £225,000. The parish of Compton Bishop's portion of that total was to be £4,500. One wonders what Herculean efforts went into fund raising to achieve such a sum fifty one years ago. It would be a daunting prospect even today. How much money was in fact raised is unclear but one assumes it must have been near the target when Lord Kindersley, President of the National Saving

Committee, wrote to Axbridge Rural District Council to say that the area had adopted HMS Goathland.

HMS Goathland was a Type III Hunt Class Destroyer laid down in 1941 and launched in 1942. She was to do convoy escort duties in the English Channel, the Atlantic, the North Sea and the Mediterranean. In 1943 Goathland and HMS Albrighton were involved in an attack on a German convoy and after a ninety minute battle the two destroyers were able to claim the sinking of an Italian merchant ship and an armed trawler. HMS Albrighton was badly damaged with many casualties but HMS Goathland received only minor damage.

In June 1944 Goathland was a headquarters ship at the Normandy invasion. She remained just off "Sword" beach controlling movements between the transports and the beaches. Once the beachhead was established she went some miles out to sea where she remained for three weeks acting as control for returning convoys by day and making protective sweeps at night.

HMS Goathland struck a mine on 24th July 1944 and although there were no casualties the ship was so badly damaged that repairs were not undertaken. HMS Goathland was scrapped at Troon in 1946.

The Home (now Compton House, Compton Bishop)

The Rectory (see page 40) was known as Rectory Farm by the end of the nineteenth century. In 1917 the house was to become a home for children with tuberculosis. At first there were only nineteen beds but by the 1930's the home could accommodate thirty three children with ages ranging from five to fourteen years.

An average stay at the home was seven months during which time the children were given "an open air life amidst most healthy and invigorating surroundings whilst their education continued in an open air school".

Mr. Ronald Bond, living at that time in Staplegrove, Taunton, was nine years old when he was sent to the Compton Bishop home in 1929. He had suffered pneumonia which had been treated by a bread poultice being placed on his chest several times a day. Despite being dosed each day with cod liver oil spooned out of a seven pound tin he failed to thrive. It was therefore decided he should go to The Home at Compton Bishop. His mother took him to the train and he travelled alone under the care of the guard to Weston-super-Mare. There he was met by a lady in a pony and trap and taken to begin one years stay at The Home. Talking of his time at the home sixty four years later he recalls a simple life with lots of exercise and lots of filling food! He says he has never been ill since and thinks his stay at the home made him very strong.

On 3rd October 1936 the Minister of Health, Sir Kinsley Wood, visited The Home and was shown around by the matron Miss Alice Bryan. The Minister was clearly impressed with what he saw saying that "here at Compton Bishop Home you have a real and successful attempt made to give real home surroundings."[19] The minister learnt that by the end of 1935 five hundred and fifty nine children had been treated at the Home and over eighty percent were perfectly well. These results the Minister said were "extremely fine".

Between 1938 and 1957 the matron was Miss Violet Gunton. The Home was now under the control of Somerset County Council. When interviewed in 1992 Miss Violet Gunton, then aged ninety, said that the Home aimed to help children at risk of tuberculosis by providing a healthy lifestyle and good food. She added that poor nourishment was a major factor in the ill health of many of the children.

The children were given plenty of exercise and they spent as much time as possible out of doors. Even their afternoon nap was taken out of doors in all weathers lying on low wooden framed beds which they called stretchers. "Windows were never closed at The Home" said Miss Gunton "If it rained the rain came in, if it snowed the snow came in".

The children had a healthy diet with lots of milk, supplied by Bourton Farm. The gardens, looked after by Frank Parramore, provided fresh vegetables and there were also plum and apple trees.

The Home closed in 1957. Some of the former residents return to Compton Bishop from time to time. Most find it hard to recognise the house but they all remember the Mulberry tree in the garden that provided the jam for the Home and whose juicy fruit dropped on to passers-by staining clothes, children's bodies and matron's crisp white uniform!.

The story of Compton Bishop and Cross was published in 1994 but the story does not end there. It continues with more waiting to be discovered. So, as well as giving enjoyment, I hope this book may encourage others to research further into Compton Bishop and Cross or their ancestors or the house in which they live thereby enhancing our knowledge of the area and the people who lived there.

▲ 37. Mrs Slim, matron at Webbington House giving the evacuees their medicine.

38. Evacuees at Webbington House with Mr H. Tiarks. ▼

▲ 39. The Home. Circa 1930's — now Compton House.

40. Children at The Home. Circa 1930's. ▼

▲ 41. Miss Alice Bryan (centre) matron at The Home. Circa 1930's.

▲ 42. Outside Moorland Farm.

43. The man in the cart is Jim Hardwidge, "the complete farm worker". ▼

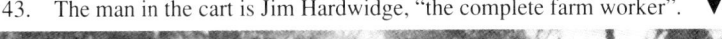

▲ 44. The Vincent family who lived at Moorland Farm from 1919–1959. Bertha and George Vincent with children (L to R) Jack, Kenneth and Donald

45. Jim Hardwidge with a ram outside Moorland Farm. ▼

▲ 46. HMS Goathland. Circa 1942.

47. The famous topiary, Cross. ▼

▲ 48. George Caple with his brother Charles on the left.

49. George Caple with Mr Skinner's stallion, "Mark Eadon Loyal Harold" probably outside the Lamb Inn, Lower Weare. ▼

▲ 50. Cross showing The New Inn before the new road was built. Circa 1925.

51. Cross near The White Hart Inn. Circa 1925. ▼

Appendix A

SURNAMES

Some of the surnames associated with Compton Bishop and Cross over several generations.

Amesbury	Hooper
Andrews	Isgar
Baden	Lukins
Burdge	Millard
Caple	Parsons
Channon	Pim/Pym
Collings	Pople
Day	Sevier
Escott	Stark
Fowles	Tilley
Fry	Toogood
Gadd	Trew
Ham	Vowles
Hase/Harse	Wickham
Hardwich/Hardwidge	

Appendix B

CENSUS INFORMATION

1811

Houses: 74 inhabited by 92 families, 1 being built, 1 uninhabited.

Occupations: 15 agriculture, 21 trade or manufacture, 56 other.

Population Count

Date	Male	Female	Total
1801			391
1811	229	255	484
1821			513
1831			554
1841			802
1851			795
1861			663
1871			655
1881			551
1891			496
1901	177	173	350
1911	187	184	371
1921	202	250	452
1931	206	229	435
1951	184	234	418
1961	196	231	427
1971	216	273	489
1981			514

LIST OF PHOTOGRAPHS

1. Aerial view of Cross and Wavering Down.
2. Meandering rhyne behind Riverton House that follows the old parish boundary.
3. The mooring stone now lying in a garden in Compton Bishop.
4. Compton Bishop, showing Dunnett Farm.
5. Wavering Down and Crook Peak.
6. The gold bracelet found in Cross in 1898.
7. Kingswood. The old boundary bank with its pollarded limes is visible on the right.
8. View of Compton Bishop from Crook Peak.
9. William Prowse memorial in Axbridge church.
10. Thomas Prowse, thought to be by Thomas Gainsborough.
11. Elizabeth Prowse, wife of Thomas Prowse, thought to be by Thomas Gainsborough.
12. Elizabeth Mordaunt (nee Prowse) by Thomas Hudson.
13. Anna Prowse memorial in Axbridge church.
14. Hatch Court near Taunton designed by Thomas Prowse.
15. Turnpike marker near Brent Knoll.
16. The toll house at Horsington, Somerset.
17. Part of the old coach road near The Crown at Churchill.
18. Manor Farm at Cross formally the King's Arms Inn.
19. The New Inn, Cross. Note the Starkey, Knight and Ford sign on the end wall.
20. The road from Shute Shelve Hill circa 1925. Now the A38.
21. The White Hart Inn, Cross.
22. Two sides of a pub token issued by the White Hart Hotel (Inn).
23. Cross, showing Moorland Farm and The White Hart.
24. Manor Farm, Compton Bishop.
25. The Cedars, Doctor Wade's home for many years.
26. Brewery Farm, all that remains of the Brewery at Cross.
27. Cross, the village shop can be seen on the right. Date unknown.
28. St. Andrews church Compton Bishop.
29. The bells of St. Andrews church prior to being re-hung in 1938.
30. Honeysuckle Cottage, Compton Bishop.
31. The quarry, Cross.

32. Doctor Arthur Leche.
33& The Tilley family outside Compton House Axbridge. Date of
34. pictures unknown.
35. Cross, Manor Farm and Cross Lane lined with elm trees. Date unknown.
36. Board of Guardians Axbridge Union Workhouse. 1930.
37. Mrs. Slim, matron at Webbington house giving the evacuees their medicine.
38. Evacuees at Webbington House with Mr. H. Tiarks.
39. The Home, circa 1930s now Compton House.
40. Children at The Home circa 1930s.
41. Miss Alice Bryan matron at The Home circa 1930s.
42. Outside Moorland Farm.
43. The man in the cart is Jim Hardwidge "the complete farmworker".
44. The Vincent family who lived at Moorland Farm from 1919-1959. Bertha and George Vincent with children (LtoR) Jack, Kenneth and Donald.
45. Jim Hardwidge with a ram outside Moorland Farm.
46. HMS Goathland. Circa 1942.
47. The celebrated topiary, Cross.
48. George Caple with his brother Charles on the left. The other man is thought to be his brother in law.
49. George Caple with Mr. Skinner's stallion "Mark Eadon Loyal Harold" probably outside the Lamb Inn at Lower Weare.
50. Cross showing the New Inn before the new road was built. Circa 1925.
51. Cross near the White Hart Inn circa 1925.

NOTES

1. Hythes and Bowes; Aspects of River Transport in Somerset. V E J Russet - Waterfront Archeology. Edited by G L Gould (CBA Research Report 741991 60 -66)
2. Geology of the County around Wells and Cheddar by G W Green. HMSO1965
3. Heart of Mendip by F A Knight
4. Information supplied by Bristol Water
5. The Mordaunts by Elizabeth Hamilton. Heinemann 1965. The Old House at Walton by Elizabeth Hamilton. Michael Russel 1988
6. Royal Archives, Windsor Castle; Miss Christine Ingram, Assistant Registrar. 1988
7. The Dickens House Museum. David Parker, Curator. 1988
8. Coleridge and Wordsworth in the West Country by Tom Mayberry. Allan Sutton 1992
9. Somerset Public House Tokens by Steve Minnitt, J Burnell and A J H Gunstone, Somerset County Council Library Services
10. Tom Brown's Schooldays by Thomas Hughes
11. Bridgewater in the later days - by Rev Arthur Powell. 1908
12. Guide to Compton Bishop Church
13. Recollections of old Taunton - by Edward Goldsworthy. 1883
14. Bristol 5th Clause and Penny Posts1795-1840 by Ian M Warn published by The Postal History Society and The Bristol Philatelic Society. 1980
15. A History of Shopping by Dorothy Davis. Routledge Kagan Paul. 1966
16. Peasant Life in the West of England by Francis George Heath. 1880
17. A History of Croydon, volume 1 by Muriel McGivern. Melway Pub Ltd
18. A Story of our villages - produced by Compton Bishop and Cross WI. 1953
19. From a newspaper report - Somersetshire Herald. 3.10. 1936

BIBLIOGRAPHY

Ackland,	Thomas Dyke and William Sturge. - The Farming of Somerset. - John Murray 1851.
Addison,	Sir William. - Old Roads of England. - Batsford 1980.
Albert,	William. - The Turnpike Road System in England 1663-1840. - Cambridge United Press 1972.
Anderson,	R. C. and J. M. Quicksilver. - A Hundred Years of Coaching 1750 - 1850. - David and Charles 1973.
Aston,	Michael - Editor. - Aspects of the Mediaeval Landscape of Somerset. - Somerset County Council 1988.
Atthill,	Robin. - Old Mendip. - David and Charles 1964.
Billingsley,	John. - Agriculture in Somerset - 1795.
Brown,	Martyn. - Australia Bound! - Ex Libris Press 1988.
Burnett,	John. - Plenty and Want - Thomas Nelson 1966.
Carley,	James P. - Glastonbury Abbey - The Holy House at the Head of the Moors. - Adventurous - Boydell Press 1988.
Census returns -	1841 to 1891.
Chuk,	Florence. - The Somerset Years. - Pennard Hill Publications, Ballerat, Victoria, Australia.
Clear,	Charles R. - John Palmer, Mail Coach Pioneer. - Blandford 1955.
Clinker,	C. R. - The Cheddar Valley Railway. - Extract from the Railway Magazine 1950.
Colvin,	Howard. - A biographical dictionary of British Architects 1600 -1840. - John Murray 1978.
Copeland,	John. - Roads and their traffic 1750 - 1850. - David and Charles 1968.
Davis,	Dorothy. - A History of Shopping. - Routledge Kegan Paul 1966.
Dickinson,	F. H. - The Banwell Charters. - S.A.N.H.S.
Directories	Pigots, Kellys, Hunts, Morris's, Slaters
Dunning,	Robert W. - Christianity in Somerset. - Somerset County Council 1975.

Dunning,	Robert. - A history of Somerset. - Somerset Libraries 1978.
Fiennes,	Celia. - Diary of Celia Fiennes - 1695.
Goldsworthy,	Edward. - Recollections of Old Taunton 1883.
Green,	G W. - Geology of the country around Wells and Cheddar. - H.M.S.O.
Hamilton,	Bernard. - Religion in the Mediaeval West - Edward Arnold 1986.
Hamilton,	Elizabeth. - The Mordaunts - Hienemann 1965.
Hamilton,	Elizabeth. - The Old House at Walton. - Michael Russell 1988.
Heath,	Francis George. - Peasant Life in the West of England. 1880.
Hembry,	Phyllis. - The Bishops of Bath and Wells 1540 - 1640. - Athlone Press 1967.
Howitt,	William. - Rural Life of England 1838.
Hughes,	Thomas. - Tom Brown's Schooldays.
Kay,	George F. - Royal Mail. - Rockcliff Publishing 1957.
Knight,	F. A. - Heart of Mendip. - Chatsford House Press Limited 1971 (First Published 1915).
Lawrence,	Berta. - Coleridge and Wordsworth in Somerset. - David and Charles 1970.
Locke's	Survey of Somerset 1795/1806.
Longmate,	Norman. - The Workhouse. - Maurice Temple Smith 1974.
Lovett,	Maurice. - Brewing and Breweries. - Shire Publications 1981.
Minnitt,	Steve., J. Burnell and A. J. H. Gunstone. - Somerset Public House Tokens. - Somerset County Council Library Service 1985.
Mayberry,	Tom. - Coleridge and Wordsworth in the West Country. - Allan Sutton 1992.
McGivern,	Muriel. - A History of Croydon. - Melway Publishing Pty Ltd, Victoria, Australia.
Middlebrook,	Martin. - The First Day on the Somme. - Allen Lane for Penguin Press 1971.

Mingay,	G E. - Rural Life in Victorian England. - Heinemann 1977.
Mountfield,	David. - The Coaching Age. - Robert Hale and Co. 1976.
Namier,	Sir Lewis and John Brooke. - The History of Parliament. The House of Commons 1754 - 1790. - HMSO 1964.
Pevsner,	Nicholas. - Buildings of England. - Penguin Books 1 1958.
Pooley,	Charles. - Old Stone Crosses of Somerset.
Powell,	Rev Arthur. - Bridgewater in the later days - 1908.
Reader,	W. J. - McAdam, The McAdam family and the Turnpike Road 1798 - 1861. - Heinemann.
Russett,	V. E. J. - Waterfront Archaeology. Hythes and Bows. Aspects of River Transport in Somerset. - Edited by G. L. Good et al (CBA Research report 741991 60 - 66).
Rutter,	John. - The County of Somerset. 1828.
Rutter,	John. - The Westonian Guide. 1829.
Shorrocks,	D M M and G T Davies. - Notes and Queries for Somerset and Dorset, Vol. xxxii.

Somerset Archaeological Society. - Report of a Survey of turnpike roads.

Somerset County Council. - Regional report prepared for Somerset County Council.

Somerset County Council. - Somerset sites and monuments record.

Warn,	Ian M. - Bristol 5th Clause and Penny Posts - 1793 - 1840. - The Postal History Society, Bristol Philatelic Society, 1980.
Webb,	Sidney and Beatrice. - The Story of the Kings Highway. - Frank Cass and Co. Ltd 1963.
Wigfield,	M A. - The Monmouth Rebels 1685. - Compiled by W. MacDonald. Somerset Record Society, Vol. 79 (1985).
Williams,	Michael. - The draining of the Somerset Levels - Oxford University Press 1970.

Women's Institute of Compton Bishop and Cross - The story of our villages, l953.

INDEX

Acland, Dyke, 46, 48, 53, 58, 66
Allotments, 20, 66 - 67
Amesbury, Henry, 75
Apprentices, 69 - 70
Arbour nursing home, 24, 58
Army Remount Centre, 81
Axbridge, 3, 6, 9, 16 - 18, 39, 44, 47, 51, 53, 60 - 61, 64, 71 - 75, 82, 84 - 85
Axbridge and West Mendip Friendly Society, 75
Axbridge Church, 17 - 18, 51
Axbridge Union, 71
Axe, 6 - 7
A38, 24, 37, 61, 82

Badgworth, 8, 15, 17, 19 - 20, 54, 58, 82
Banwell, 4, 13 - 16, 60
Banwell, Ada, 54
Bidwell Family, The, 69
Bilbie, W. W., 39
Billingsley, John, 8, 44 - 45, 63
Bishop of Bath and Wells, 3, 9, 18, 76
Blacksmith, 53, 56 - 57
Bloody Assizes, 26
Bourton, 3
Bourton Coombe, 5, 10
Bourton Farm, 42, 52, 81, 88
Bowden, John, 65, 75
Bowles, Louisa, 54
Bracelet, gold, 8
Brent Knoll, 8, 24, 28
Brewery, 59 - 61, 81 - 82
Brewery Farm, 46, 61
Bridgwater, 24, 28, 33, 50, 69
Bridle Cottage, 62
Bristol Trust, The, 24, 81
Bryan, Miss Alice, 87
Burdge, John, 29
Burdge, Richard, 57
Burdge, Samuel, 57
Butts Batch, 53

Callow children, The, 70
Caple, Charles and Rebecca, 42
Caple, Edward, 74
Caple, William, 16, 74

Carpenter, 43, 57 - 58
Carrier, 35, 57 - 58, 64 - 65
Caves, 5, 37
Cedars, The, 50 - 51, 57
Chagford (Devon), 16
Channon, Charles, 61
Channon, Robert, 58
Channon, Walter, 45
Cheddar, 9, 28, 47, 56, 60 - 61, 71
Cheddar Valley Line, 47
Cheddar Yeo, 6 - 7
Cheese production, 48
Cider, 46, 59 - 60, 65 - 66, 83
Cleevehead, 45, 50, 63
Coaching, 28 - 30, 34, 37, 56
Coleridge, Samuel, 27 - 28
Collings, 59 - 61
Combe Hay, 46
Compton Bishop Farm, 7
Compton Bishop School, 54 - 56, 81, 83, 84 -85
Compton House, Axbridge, 39, 53
Compton House, Compton Bishop, 40, 86
Congresbury, 13 - 14, 16, 31, 38
Constabulary, Somerset, 62
Court, The, 56 - 58
Cray, William, 54
Crook Peak, 4 - 5
Cross Lane, 10
Cross Memorial Hall, 24, 85
Cross Moor, 43, 81
Crossways House, 52
Crown Inn, The, 25
Cyclist's Touring Club, 35

Davey, Thomas, 64
Dettingen, Battle of, 41
Dickens, Charles, 26 - 27
Drainage, 6 - 8
Ducod, 14
Dudoc, 13
Duke of Somerset, 14 - 15
Dunnett Farm, 10

97

Elizabeth I, 15, 69
Emery, James, 56 - 57
Emigrants, 76
Enclosure, 43 - 44
Evacuees, 83

Flint axe heads, 37
Fowles, Williams, 58
Fry, John, 39
Fry, Peter, 44

Gadd, Samuel, 44
Giso, 14
Glastonbury, 7, 38
Glastonbury Thorn, 85
Godby, Silas, 62
Grafton Park, Northamptonshire, 18
Guardians of the Poor, 70
Gunton, Miss Violet, 84, 87 - 88
GWR, 47

Haise, Thomas, 54
Hardwidge, Samuel and John, 76
Hardwitch, James, 74
Harse, William, 56
Hatch Court, 19
Havisham, Miss, 26 - 27
Hellier, David, 57
Henning, Robert, 39 - 40
Henry VIII, 14
Highwaymen, 31
HMS Goathland, 86
Holts of Burnham, 61
Home Guard, 60, 82
Home, The, 84, 86 - 88
Honeysuckle Cottage, 65
Hooper, Levi and Hannah, 42
Howell, Mrs, 84

Jones, James, 61
Jones. Samuel, 74

Kaley, John, 83
Keen, Louisa, 64 - 65
Kings Arms, 25 - 26, 29, 33 - 34
Kings Wood, 9

Leche, Dr. Arthur, 51, 80
Leche, Victor, 80
Lewis, Hester, 52
Lime kiln, 63
Littlehales, Reverend, 42, 49 - 50

Longbourne, 54
Lower Weare, 7, 24, 56, 81, 84
Loxton, 3, 39, 61, 79

Macadam, John, 24, 28
Mail coach, 32 - 33
Manor Court, The, 26, 49
Manor Farm, Compton Bishop, 39, 53
Manor Farm, Cross, 9, 25, 29, 56, 61 - 62
Market gardening, 46, 58
Marshall. Richard, 62
Medlam, James, 58
Mercer, Syd, 83
Merry, Florence, 43
Milestones, 24
Mill, 6 - 7, 9, 46
Millage, Ralph, 84
Millard, James, 29
Millard, Onisephorus, 71
Mills, William, 50, 62
Monksilver, 46
Mooring stone, 3
Moorland Farm, 57, 83
Mordaunt, 5, 18, 20 - 21, 25, 44 - 45, 48,
    61, 63, 66, 68, 76
Mordaunt, Elizabeth, 20

New Inn, The, 25 - 26, 34
Newton House, 26 - 27, 50
Newton, Sir Henry, 5, 15
Newtown, 43, 47, 58
Norwell. George, 61

Orchards, 46, 77, 83

Paine George, 62
Palmer, John, 32
Parramore, Frank, 88
Parsons, Elizabeth, 52
Parsons, James, 46
Police house, 62
Poor house, 38 - 39, 64, 67, 69 - 70
Poor Law Act, 67, 70
Pople, John, 47, 58
Pople, William, 57
Porch, Thomas and Eliza, 42
Post Office, 32 - 33, 61 - 62, 64
Postman, 61 - 62
Pound, The, 45, 85
Prisoners of war, 83
Prowse estate, 9, 19

Prowse, John, 15, 17 - 18, 44
Prowse, Thomas, 9, 18 - 20
Prowse, William, 15 - 17, 25, 37, 44
Public house checks, 29
Pumping station, 8
Pyther, Martha, 74

Quarries, 5, 15, 79
Queen Victoria, 26 - 27

Rackley, 3
Rectory, The, 40, 49, 86
Riverside Farm, 7
Riverton House, 7
Road, Medieval, 7
Road, Old Coach, 7, 24, 32, 45 - 46, 56, 82
Road, Webbington, 45
Rosewood, 9
Salisbury, James & Elizabeth, 72
Saw mill, 9
Say, John, 58 - 59
Shop, 53, 56, 63 - 64
Shop keeper, 53
Shute Shelve, 5 - 6, 10, 25, 29, 31, 37, 58, 81
Slim, Mrs, 84
Spearing, William, 17
St. Andrew's Church, 38, 80
Star Inn, 25
Stark, Emma, 53, 64
Stark, William, 65 - 66
Starkey, Knight and Ford, 61
Stock, Grace, 74
Stone, Gabriel, 28
Strawberries, 4, 47

Tannery, 53, 58
Tanning, 9
Teasels, 45 - 46
Tiarks, Herman, 79

Tollhouse, 24 - 25
Toogood, William, 53
Townsend Farm, 51
Tripp, Joseph, 74
Turnpike Trusts, 23

Vernon's Lane, 53
Vestry, The, 67 - 68
Vicarage, 49, 65, 75, 83
Vowles, Charles, 64
Vowles, George Escott, 64
Vowles, James, 65, 74

Wade, Edward, 50 - 52
Walton Hall, 20 - 21
Wavering Down, 3 - 5
Weare, 8, 38, 84
Webbington, 3, 6, 45, 61
Webbington Farm, 4
Webbington House, 79 - 80, 83
Webbington Road, 45
Wells, 7 - 8, 13 - 14, 16, 18 - 19, 26, 34, 38 - 39
Weston-super-Mare, 16, 34, 61, 65, 71, 82 - 83, 87
Wheelwright, 56 - 57
Whitbreads, 61
White Hart, The, 25 - 26, 30, 33 - 35, 45, 56 - 57, 62
Wickham, George, 52
Wickham, William, 39
Winscombe, 16, 39, 79
Withy beds, 46
Wordsworth, William, 28
Workhouse, 3, 70 - 75
World War I, 65, 80
World War II, 60, 82

Yews, The, 79

99